VISUAL ART AND SELF-CONSTRUCTION

Crosscurrents

Exploring the development of European thought through engagements with the arts, humanities, social sciences and sciences

Series Editor
Christopher Watkin, Monash University

Editorial Advisory Board
Andrew Benjamin
Martin Crowley
Simon Critchley
Frederiek Depoortere
Oliver Feltham
Patrick ffrench
Christopher Fynsk
Kevin Hart
Emma Wilson

Titles available in the series
Difficult Atheism: Post-Theological Thinking in Alain Badiou, Jean-Luc Nancy and Quentin Meillassoux
Christopher Watkin
Politics of the Gift: Exchanges in Poststructuralism
Gerald Moore
Unfinished Worlds: Hermeneutics, Aesthetics and Gadamer
Nicholas Davey
The Figure of This World: Agamben and the Question of Political Ontology
Mathew Abbott
The Becoming of the Body: Contemporary Women's Writing in French
Amaleena Damlé
Philosophy, Animality and the Life Sciences
Wahida Khandker
The Event Universe: The Revisionary Metaphysics of Alfred North Whitehead
Leemon B. McHenry
Sublime Art: Towards an Aesthetics of the Future
Stephen Zepke
Mallarmé and the Politics of Literature: Sartre, Kristeva, Badiou, Rancière
Robert Boncardo
Animal Writing: Storytelling, Selfhood and the Limits of Empathy
Danielle Sands
Music, Philosophy and Gender in Nancy, Lacoue-Labarthe, Badiou
Sarah Hickmott
The Desert in Modern Literature and Philosophy: Wasteland Aesthetics
Aidan Tynan
Visual Art and Self-Construction
Katrina Mitcheson

Visit the Crosscurrents website at www.edinburghuniversitypress.com/series-crosscurrents.html

VISUAL ART AND SELF-CONSTRUCTION

Katrina Mitcheson

EDINBURGH
University Press

Edinburgh University Press is one of the leading university presses in the UK. We publish academic books and journals in our selected subject areas across the humanities and social sciences, combining cutting-edge scholarship with high editorial and production values to produce academic works of lasting importance. For more information visit our website: edinburghuniversitypress.com

Edinburgh University Press Ltd
The Tun – Holyrood Road, 12(2f) Jackson's Entry, Edinburgh EH8 8PJ

First published in hardback by Edinburgh University Press 2021

Typeset in 10.5/13 Sabon by
Servis Filmsetting Ltd, Stockport, Cheshire,
and printed and bound by CPI Group (UK) Ltd, Croydon, CR0 4YY

A CIP record for this book is available from the British Library

ISBN 978 0 7486 9367 2 (hardback)
ISBN 978 0 3995 1118 6 (paperback)
ISBN 978 0 7486 9 68 9 (webready PDF)
ISBN 978 1 4744 0479 2 (epub)

Contents

Series Editor's Preface

Two or more currents flowing into or through each other create a turbulent crosscurrent, more powerful than its contributory flows and irreducible to them. Time and again, modern European thought creates and exploits crosscurrents in thinking, remaking itself as it flows through, across and against discourses as diverse as mathematics and film, sociology and biology, theology, literature and politics. The work of Gilles Deleuze, Jacques Derrida, Slavoj Žižek, Alain Badiou, Bernard Stiegler and Jean-Luc Nancy, among others, participates in this fundamental remaking. In each case disciplines and discursive formations are engaged, not with the aim of performing a predetermined mode of analysis yielding a 'philosophy of x', but through encounters in which thought itself can be transformed. Furthermore, these fundamental transformations do not merely seek to account for singular events in different sites of discursive or artistic production but rather to engage human existence and society as such, and as a whole. The cross-disciplinarity of this thought is therefore neither a fashion nor a prosthesis; it is simply part of what 'thought' means in this tradition.

Crosscurrents begins from the twin convictions that this remaking is integral to the legacy and potency of European thought, and that the future of thought in this tradition must defend and develop this legacy in the teeth of an academy that separates and controls the currents that flow within and through it. With this in view, the series provides an exceptional site for bold, original and opinion-changing monographs that actively engage European thought in this fundamentally cross-disciplinary manner, riding existing crosscurrents and creating new ones. Each book in the series explores the different ways in which European thought develops through its engagement with disciplines across the arts, humanities, social sciences and sciences, recognising that the community of scholars working with this thought is itself spread across diverse faculties. The object of the series is therefore nothing less than to examine and carry forward the unique legacy of European thought as an inherently and irreducibly cross-disciplinary enterprise.

Christopher Watkin
Cambridge
February 2011

Acknowledgements

I would like to thank my colleagues in philosophy at the University of the West of England for their encouragement and for providing an atmosphere of philosophical discussion. In particular, I would like to thank Iain Hamilton Grant, who read the manuscript in draft and provided invaluable feedback and suggestions throughout the project. I would also like to thank Barry Barker for his enthusiasm at the project's beginning and suggestions of artists to discuss. Matthew Dennis, Alison Assiter and David Roden also offered suggestions and engaged in valuable discussion. I have appreciated opportunities to present and discuss the work in development at visiting research seminars at the philosophy departments of the University of Warwick and the University of Dundee. I would also like to thank the reviewers at Edinburgh University Press for their suggestions and the series editor Christopher Watkin for his comments. Critical input and creative stimulation through sharing ideas with colleagues has been essential to the project's development.

For my parents, Martin and Muriel, who cultivated my love of art
from childhood. And for my aunt, Christie, who helped me to expand
my knowledge of art in new directions.

Introduction

When confronted with the most brutal of Francisco de Goya y Lucientes's prints from his series *The Disasters of War*, repulsion fights fascination. Originally titled *Fatal Consequences of Spain's Bloody War with Bonaparte, and Other Emphatic Caprices*, Goya's series of gruelling images of rape, murder and mutilated corpses was created between 1810 and 1820 but not published until 1863. These prints convey the horror of war, but horror is not all we feel when looking at them. To see an image such as plate no. 37, *This is Worse* (*Esto es Peor*, Figure I.1), is complex. Perhaps the most immediate response to the sight of the armless man, impaled on the branch of a tree, is disgust. We might also feel pity for this individual and the victims of war he represents. Some of us will feel anger towards the perpetrators, amazement at their cruelty or despair at a world in which such atrocities take place. We may not rest at the level of a distant observer of the crimes of history. Stare at it too long and we might identify our own fleshy and vulnerable bodies with the violated corpse displayed on the tree, feeling anxiety in the face of our openness to injury, death and pain, and relief that this body is not our own. Perhaps we may feel a twinge in corresponding limbs in our own body or feel nauseous. For some, there might be present an element of sadistic pleasure and bodily excitement at this testimony of another's pain and powerlessness. Or again, this encounter may contain something that we cannot articulate, that does not find a fit in our list of emotional vocabulary. While reactions to the artwork will not be the same for everyone, nor will they be the same for any one of us with each encounter; they are likely to be complicated.

What can one make of such a complexity of feelings in the face of Goya's work? When I examine my personal experience of the artwork, I find I am capable of feeling a range of sometimes opposing, sometimes unexpected, often confused and opaque feelings simultaneously. I learn

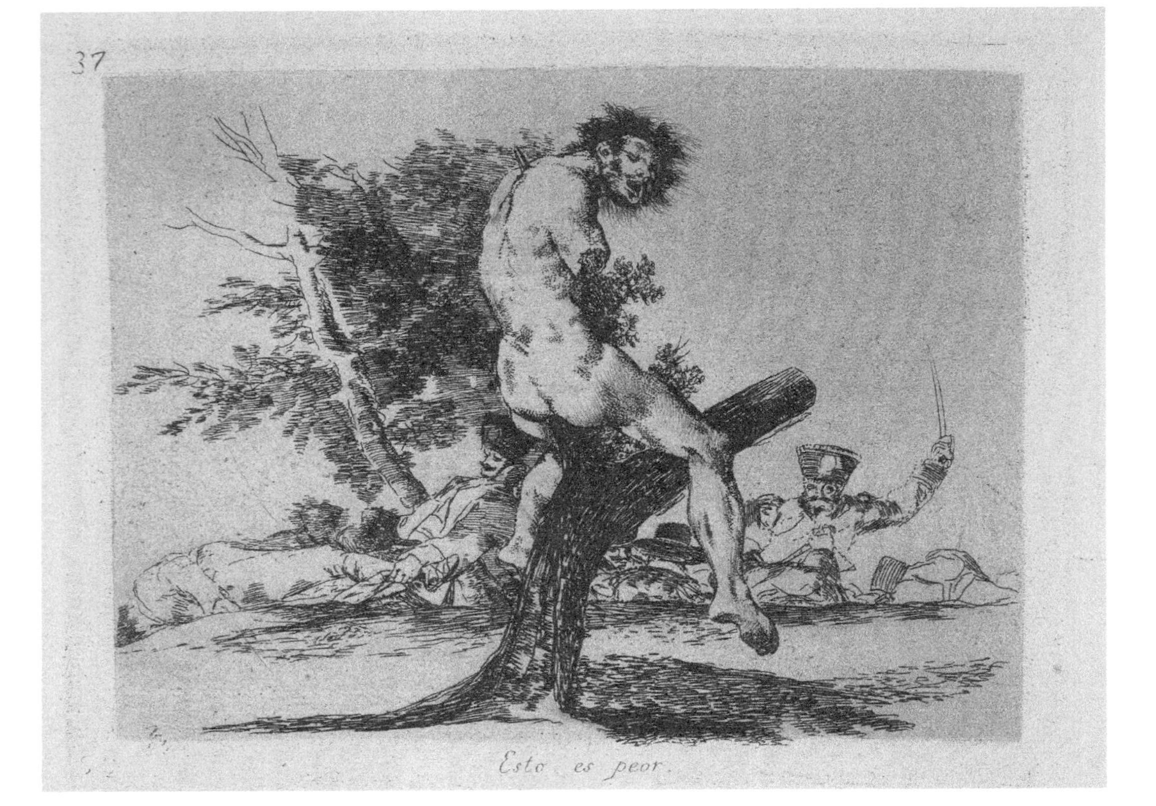

I.1 Francisco de Goya y Lucientes, *This is Worse (Esto es peor)*, completed between 1812–1815, published 1863, plate 37 of the *Disasters of War* series, etching, lavis and drypoint on paper, 15.5 × 20.5 cm

that I can be pulled in different directions and can have competing impulses and contradictory reactions. I realise that I do not always understand, or want to condone, my own feelings. My engagement with these artworks reveals a multiplicity of feelings and impulses some of which may be difficult to control, some obscure, others surprising or even repellent to me. This not only informs me that I am complex, but challenges the very idea of who 'I' am.

In the face of this complexity, I still talk about these varied and even antagonistic reactions to an artwork as being 'my' reactions. Dan Zahavi argues that all our experiences, whether the sensations of warmth and flavour when we take a sip of coffee, or a sense of horror when looking at the Goya prints, have a 'first personal-givenness' to them (Zahavi 2007: 188). On Zahavi's account, the experience I have of horror when looking at Goya's etchings is not reducible to the quality of horror. Rather it is characterised as horror that is being experienced by me; that is as *my* being horrified. Zahavi suggests that in this experience we already find a 'minimal experiential self' (2007: 193).[1] Zahavi acknowledges that we go beyond this minimal self if we understand ourselves as characters who develop across time (2007: 193). I want to argue, however, that we go beyond any such minimal self already when we interpret different feelings or reactions as implying a tension within a particular self. The experience of internal conflict already introduces the interpretation of personality or character that can feel conflicted. The very notion of tension and of the complexity of feelings, which I suggested is felt in looking at *The Disasters of War*, requires a degree of unity, which need not be prior to but can be taken to emerge from these interactions. The interpretation of feeling torn, confused, pulled in different directions at least implies that the different feelings or impulses occurring interact with each other. They do not exist in isolation; they compete, form alliances, modify each other and create new composites. The idea of a minimal experiential self does not account for these interactions, but neither does it address the challenge to our assumptions regarding the unity of the self that such complexity presents. Accounting for complexity, conflict and tension, both assumes some kind of unity that goes beyond the minimal self and raises the question of what such unity involves, and how it arises and is maintained.

Friedrich Nietzsche suggests that the idea of a unified self, the very idea of a subject, who does and is done to, is a 'fiction' (Nietzsche 1988: vol. 12, 315). This fiction, on Nietzsche's analysis, tends to deny the complexity, and unsettledness, that he believes we will find when we pay proper attention to what we call 'our' experiences. This does not mean however, that we should simply discard the idea of a self, rather than incorporate into it the recognition that the self is a construction that is inherently complicated and unstable such that there is no given or final unity.[2] As Paul Ricoeur notes, personal pronouns demonstrate a 'tenacity', which resists elimination in impersonal description (1992: 138–9). In speaking of connections between experiences and of internal conflict we employ personal pronouns because we understand the connections and tensions as being experienced by a self which can experience various degrees of harmony and tension. A self that is unified in the sense of having a character, rather than being merely a disparate collection of different motives or impulses, is integral to our understanding of our actions, experiences and relationships. A self that is unified in the sense of having a continuous history, such that our past actions, current decisions and future hopes and plans are connected, is a presupposition in any future-orientated projects. The challenge is, therefore, can we reconcile a self that is unified in this way with the diversity and mutability we encounter in experience?

I want to argue in this book that our encounters with artworks challenge and undermine the assumption that there is a simple or fixed self, but also maintain that there is a complex and constructed self which achieves at least a partial, if changing and vulnerable, unity, one that impermanently incorporates diversity and tensions. The question, which I will be exploring throughout this book, therefore becomes: how is such a self, which allows us to understand this diversity as in some sense unified, constructed? I will argue that the self is established through various interpretative processes and practices and is thus usefully characterised as what Michel Foucault terms a hermeneutics of the self (Foucault 1993). I will suggest that we can understand this as incorporating bodily processes and the interpretation of drives, as elucidated in different ways by Nietzsche and Sigmund Freud, as well as the various acts of knowing and describing the self, and practices which work on the self, of the sort that Foucault catalogues.

If the self is not only known but in fact constructed through interpretation, then the question arises of what is being interpreted and what is doing the interpreting? The science of hermeneutics is rooted in the exegesis of religious texts, and there is thus the danger that hermeneutic approaches to the self rely on an overly literal model of the self as the interpretation of a 'text' in the sense of a written text such as a work of literature. This is evidenced by the prevalence of narrative theories of the self,[3] which take the literary structure of narrative as the paradigm for the creation of a self through interpretation, and in some popular interpretations of thinkers of self-construction, such as Nehamas's reading of Nietzsche (Nehamas 1985).

But if we construe the hermeneutics of the self along the lines of the interpretation of a written text then there is a temptation to posit the idea of an underlying text as an underlying truth. This idea of text can then serve various functions. Throughout *The History of Sexuality; The Will to Knowledge* (1978), Foucault elaborates the concern that various practices such as confession, whether religious, psychoanalytic or literary, are held to be revealing a hidden self, mediated in various ways that require interpretation. Foucault warns us that this hidden self is used both to legitimise these practices and to limit the forms of acceptable selfhood available. In developing an account of the hermeneutics of the self we should thus aim to avoid falling into this trap of positing a 'hidden self' in which the self is analogous to a text which has already been written, waiting to be interpreted or revealed. But even if we guard against this assumption of an underlying self, and we understand the hermeneutics of the self as working to construct rather than reveal the self, there are still dangers in positing the hermeneutics of the self in terms of the interpretation of a text.

In relying on the analogy between hermeneutics of the self and hermeneutics of the written text, we reduce the ways in which we express and form selves, to linguistic activity, or to activities that could be translated into language. Indeed, many philosophers, such as Ricoeur, go further and take their understanding of self-awareness and agency from a specific literary structure – that of narrative. This narrative understanding is particularly useful in making sense of the unity of the self through time. It allows us to see ourselves as agents in the context of our pasts and futures. If we see our lives in terms of narrative then our past experiences and actions can be seen to shape our characters, which along with our future hopes and plans direct, and make sense of, our current choices. Actions, according to Ricoeur, are connected together in the way the plot of a novel is connected, and our actions are connected to our character as they would be for the hero of a novel. Thus, on this account, particular actions are given meaning, and our lives as a whole are given form, as those of a character embedded in the plot of their life. Narrative may indeed be a crucial part of self-understanding, and of how the kind of self that can have projects of knowledge, self-improvement or resistance is continually produced. A narrative model of self-construction, however, reduces the process of self-construction to emplotment, and I will argue that in doing so it overlooks the variety of ways in which we become, and can work on, selves, and offers an impoverished view of the hermeneutics of the self.

It is not only a question of what is left out by the narrative model of the self, which could then be corrected by supplementing the account it gives. My claim is that the narrative account fundamentally mis-construes the processes of self-construction. A narrative model of the hermeneutics of the self neglects the materiality, the corporeality, of processes of self-formation. In considering the range of reactions that we can have to the Goya prints it is clear that we react to the bodies depicted in a bodily way. Our materiality, our corporeality, is the condition of possibility and the limit on self-construction, and the varied processes of self-construction are bodily processes. On an understanding of the hermeneutics of the self which emphasises corporeality, it is these bodily processes, including the activity of our drives, which interpret.

In this book, I attempt to model a corporeal hermeneutics of the self as an alternative to theories of self-construction which reduce it to narrative activity or which privilege narrative at the expense of recognising the diversity of practices that do, and could, contribute to self-construction. To this end, I turn to visual or plastic art. Visual art is an imperfect term. I use it in contrast to the literary and musical arts. For historical reasons, it clusters together art forms that are primarily visual – drawings, prints, paintings – with those that use non-visual elements such as sound and touch. In my use of the term visual art I include performance, installations, video art and mixed media work which may not be visual in focus. I use visual rather than plastic art to avoid the misunderstanding of the narrow use of plastic art to refer to three-dimensional works formed through moulding plastic materials, as in ceramics or sculpture. However, it is as much the plastic as visual properties of the artworks under discussion that I will argue make visual art so helpful in understanding self-construction. A successful approach to visual art does not reduce it to symbols, which in turn reduce to the linguistic. In visual art (material) form and content do not come apart. The material of a painting, a sculpture, an installation or performance is not incidental to its meaning. The meaning emerges in a process that depends on and is constrained by its material. As Christian Lotz argues 'the process character of art' does not permit the semiotic approach to art (Lotz 2017: 33). Artworks are worked matter, but the artist must work with the limits and possibilities of particular materials. These materials have their own processes the elude the complete control of the artist. In discussing the production of visual art, we reach a better understanding of the dependence of form on material processes and can thus develop a model for understanding self-construction as a material process.

Particular artworks can also help us gain insight into the specific materiality of self-construction, namely our corporeality, and its cultural expression. Artworks, such as Goya's prints discussed above, engage the bodily drives of the audience and express the artist's drives, alerting us to the presence of their interpretative activity. As material objects, events or processes, visual art engages us as physical, sensual beings, making us more aware of our own corporeality and thus of the importance of recognising this corporeality in any account of self-construction. But as part of the cultural world which interprets this corporeality, artworks also allow us to understand the different forces and techniques which shape it. Visual art at once reveals the impossibility of understanding the body and its drives apart from cultural expression and asserts the ineliminable corporeality of our cultural expressions. Artworks can deconstruct and critique the forms of self currently available to us, revealing the various ways in which we are being constructed in the context of a particular culture. Cindy Sherman's photographs, for example, reveal the construction and limitation of female identity in terms of various feminine tropes. But art can also provide an example of how novelty can emerge from within existing materials, whether the physical materials of construction or the social and cultural resources and significations within which the artist works.

Through my discussion of particular artworks, therefore, I aim in this book to arrive at a better understanding of self-construction than that offered by narrative theories. One that is arrived at not simply by supplementing narrative but by understanding the processes of self-construction as diverse and corporeal. This is by no means the only way that we can interact with and find value in visual artworks, but if we are interested in understanding and potentially in changing ourselves, visual art offers us insights and resources to do so. Properly understanding processes of self-construction enables us in our projects of knowing and working on the self, whether these are aimed at personal well-being or at more radical challenges to the forms of selfhood available to us, providing a means of resistance to the ossified power structures in which they are implicated.

In discussing artworks by Francisco de Goya y Lucientes, Francis Bacon, Louise Bourgeois, Cindy Sherman, Sonia Boyce, Claude Cahun, ORLAN, Carolee Schneemann, Yvonne Rainer, Marina Abramović, Rebecca Horn, Mona Hatoum, Steve McQueen, Hermann Nitsch and Joseph Beuys, I am not reducing the meaning or value of their artworks to the understanding they bring to the hermeneutics of the self. Rather, I am employing their artworks as tools to understand and model a corporeal hermeneutics of the self. Given that self-construction operates in a cultural sphere and can employ representations and examples that artworks offer up to their audiences, I also understand their work as contributing to the material and thus possibilities of self-construction.

In approaching the work of these artists, I do not think there is a final meaning of their work that is reducible to the artists' interpretations. I agree with Nicholas Davey that engaging in artwork is itself a creative, dialogical process that establishes, rather than simply 'finding', complex and evolving meanings of a work through particular encounters with them (Davey 2002: 443). We can still treat the artist's intentions as an important part of establishing the meaning(s) of the work, without seeing their intentions as determinate of the meaning. As Davey suggests: 'though the self-understanding of the practitioner may be transformed by any hermeneutic engagement, that understanding remains an indispensable point of departure and return for critical reflection' (Davey 2002: 445). My discussions of artworks will thus focus on the particularity of encountering the works. But in analysing these encounters, I will draw on an understanding of the social and art historical context of the work, employ the interviews and writings of the artists, and refer to discussions of their work in the fields of art history and art theory. The insights offered on art practice and artistic works through the commentary of art theorists and historians and artists themselves open up perspectives on artworks and enrich our encounter with them, but in our encounter with it we interpret the work for ourselves. Thus, while often inspired by and intersecting with extant interpretations in the literature, it is ultimately my own interpretation of and responses to works that I employ towards an account of a corporeal hermeneutics of the self.

In Chapter 1, I put the case for why we need an account of the hermeneutics of the self. I argue for a view of the self as constructed through interpretative processes by drawing on the thought of Nietzsche, Freud and Foucault. These thinkers, while diverse, all question an idea of the self as simple and given. If there is any self for them, it stands in contrast to the idea of a fixed and unchanging substance and must allow for complexity and mutability. They share a view of the self that departs from its Cartesian connotations and must be understood instead as emerging in a historically specific process. Both Freud and Nietzsche understand the processes of self-formation or self-construction as fundamentally corporeal through the notion of active drives. The bodily drives contribute to the construction of selves through their own interpretative activity. Where these thinkers diverge is itself illuminating, and a better understanding of the problem of self-construction can be arrived at by placing them in critical dialogue; with insights into the importance of other related drives in Freud and the role of institutions in Foucault adding a useful supplement to Nietzsche's insights into the interpretative activity of drives and challenge to the idea of any simple and unified agency. Crucially, we find in these thinkers different views about what a self need, or should, look like. This disagreement on what could constitute a self, and how open its possibilities are, points to the importance of art, through which what constitutes the creation of unity out of multiplicity, and what forms of selfhood are possible, can be experimented with.

In Chapter 2, I explore in detail Ricoeur's theory of a narrative self in which he proposes that a coherent self is created through plot. Ricoeur offers a particularly sophisticated understanding of a narrative self and thus shows the advantages of this approach, which establishes a unity of experience and the possibility of agency without relying on an idea of the self as an underlying substrate. In this chapter, I suggest the need to incorporate some of Ricoeur's insights, in particular his understanding of the interaction between life and art, in which our artistic representations are only possible because of a meaningful field of actions and that field of actions is shaped and expanded by artistic representations. I also, however, set out where I think his approach is lacking, suggesting that the model of emplotment neglects corporeality and obscures the multiplicity of processes of self-construction. Narrative theory thus oversimplifies the agency involved in self-construction. While Ricoeur offers a view of the self that incorporates heterogeneous elements in a way that can accommodate ongoing change, it is ultimately reductive to see the process of self-construction entirely in terms of emplotment and the forms of possible self as able to map onto a character in a plot. Ricoeur suggests that a disintegration of plot is a disintegration of character. But the paintings of Francis Bacon remind us that the self is also threatened by bodily disintegration. We need an account of the hermeneutics of the self that can incorporate somatic and plural interpretative activities.

In Chapter 3, I employ the visual art of Louise Bourgeois towards the development of an alternative, corporeal account of self-construction. Bourgeois is an artist who foregrounds the materiality of artworks and plays with the limits and possibilities of a variety of materials. Her work highlights how material processes both enable the emergence of form and can resist the direction of formation that an artist attempts to impose. It thus – in the creation of form from out of a multiplicity of processes – offers a model of construction that can incorporate multiple agencies and a diversity of interpretations that are simultaneous rather than alternating or supplanting. Further, Bourgeois's art illustrates that material construction is irreconcilable with total authorial control because materials have their own directional tendencies. Bourgeois's work also shows us how on the one hand what is fluid can become ossified but also how emergent forms can be once more engulfed by material process. This can be seen to be mirrored in how the cultural iterations of our identity can be constraining and how our drives can overwhelm any such identity. Her work addresses the limitations of social roles and the expectations placed on women's bodies, suggesting that identity can be a trap, while also suggesting that maintaining a coherent self in the face of competing drives requires continual work or reconstruction. Visual art can operate as a technology of the self employed in working on the self but also in the task of escaping from the trap of identity.

In Chapter 4, I explore the self as a site of resistance and the role of visual art as a critical technology of the self that contributes to this resistance. As Stephen Greenblatt insists in his account of *Renaissance Self-Fashioning*, 'fashioning oneself and being fashioned by cultural institutions – family, religion, state – were intertwined' (1980: 256).[4] In this chapter, I will elaborate Foucault's understanding of power which provides a framework in which we can understand the ways in which the family, religion, state, etc., fashion us as the operation of power tactics. If Foucault is right that the form the self takes is in the context of power strategies that employ a particular form of selfhood in their operation, then refusing these forms of self can serve to challenge power orders. Many artworks interrogate the identities available to us as selves and the role of power structures in informing self-construction. For example, visual art can shed particular light on how visual structures, images and ways of seeing can form part of the context of power relations in which the self is shaped and acts. They thus reveal the varied ways beyond narrative in which the self is constructed. They can also, however, themselves operate to reinforce potentially oppressive identities, such as oppressive articulations of gender. The example of female identity provides a clear example of how artworks can both contribute to the formation of restrictive identities and operate as a tool of critique which helps to free us from being tied to them. In this chapter, I focus in particular on Cindy Sherman's *Untitled Film Stills* (1977–80). Her work demonstrates the active role the viewer plays in constructing the identity of others, and how women's identity is constrained not just by the particular tropes of femininity that images signify for us, but by its equation to image or narrative. Sherman's later work asserts the presence of bodily processes that cannot be captured in these coded forms. If artworks can serve the critical function of showing how the self is continually being constructed in diverse ways, then they can open the space for experimentation with alternative forms of construction. But how can we incorporate what eludes codification and engage in a hermeneutics of the self which does not simply reproduce a subjugated self?

In Chapter 5, I attempt to answer this question, considering how artworks can operate not only as critical technologies of the self, to employ Foucault's term (Foucault 1988: 18), but as technologies of the self that can help to develop new identities and new ways of relating to our identity which are not constraining. I discuss how re-appropriation of imagery that has been used to oppress us is insufficient, and we need to go beyond the normative assumption that identity can be reduced to image or narrative and harness bodily processes that cannot be codified in these ways. I consider how various artists, including Yvonne Rainer and Rebecca Horn, open up new perspectives on the body and allow us to unlearn bodily habits, and engage a range of senses, while other artists, such as Hermann Nitsch, seek to work on and affect our bodily drives through immersive audience experiences. Experimental engagements with the body can provide us with the means to experiment with new modes of selfhood. What emerges from these discussions is that artworks and working on the self are continually in interaction, and that critique and experimentation in one sphere create new possibilities in the other.

NOTES

1. Zahavi argues that a pre linguistic core self is the precondition of more extended notions of selfhood such as that found in narrative theories of the self (2007).
2. Indeed, I would suggest that Nietzsche radicalises rather than discards the idea of a self. Dubbing it a fiction serves the purpose of both rejecting the fixed or given self as pure fiction and reminding us that any operative notion of the self is something we create. It does not, on my reading, however, dismiss it as *mere* fiction or illusion.
3. For example, despite various important theoretical differences (crucially for Dennett the self is a useful fiction [Dennett 1992]), as Fred Vollmer sums up in his review of narrative constructions of the self: 'Dennett, Schafer, Schechtman, McAdams all agree selves are created by stories' (2005: 203). Marya Schechtman meanwhile notes that 'Alasdair MacIntyre, Charles Taylor, and Paul Ricoeur' all share the claim that selves are 'fundamentally self-interpreting beings' for whom 'leading the life of a self is taken inherently to involve understanding one's life as a narrative and enacting the narrative one sees as one's life' (2011: 395).
4. Greenblatt is not presenting a narrative theory of the self. He does not present a theory of self per se, rather than a particular and historically embedded account of self-fashioning, and he recognises, for instance, that how we

dress and comport ourselves in social situations is part of self-fashioning. In contrast to my focus, however, Greenblatt's is on language, claiming that '[s]elf-fashioning is always, though not exclusively in language' (Greenblatt 1980: 9). And his analysis of self-fashioning is conducted through studies of literature.

1. *The Self and its Vicissitudes*

INTRODUCTION

In his quest for solid foundations on which to build scientific knowledge, René Descartes employs the method of doubt, searching for a keystone that can survive the most extreme doubt and on which a secure edifice of certain principles can be rebuilt. The point of certainty he arrives at is, as is well known, the cogito: 'So, after considering everything very thoroughly, I must finally conclude that the proposition, *I am, I exist*, is necessarily true whenever it is put forward by me or conceived in my mind' (Descartes 2017: 21). From this point, Descartes moves on to argue that all that we know of this 'I' is that it is a thinking thing, concluding that:

> I am, then, in the strict sense only a thing that thinks [*res cogitans*]; that is, I am a mind, or intelligence, or intellect, or reason – words whose meaning I have been ignorant of until now. But for all that I am a thing which is real and which truly exists. But what kind of a thing? As I have just said – a thinking thing. (Descartes 2017: 22–3)

That we can know ourselves, as a thinking thing or substance [*res*], is thus taken to be unproblematic by Descartes and to imply that this thinking thing is distinct and independent. The 'I' of the cogito is a self that is reduced to conscious thinking.

An encounter with an artwork, such as Goya's etchings, with a description of which I began this book, exposes the inadequacy of an understanding of the self which is based on the cogito. First, the idea that thinking is 'pure' and open to introspection is itself put into question. Conscious thoughts, judgements about the nature of the artworks, are shown to be opaque, open to different and layered interpretations. If there is no pure thinking, then there is no basis on which to assert that there is a pure thinking thing.

Second, it is clear that a self that is reduced to conscious thinking does little work in making sense of the complexity of feelings and reactions involved in experiences such as looking at Goya's etchings. As we explored in the introduction, this encounter is complex, changeable and, crucially, it is bodily. We can feel bodily sensations in response to such artworks, from a general sense of agitation to a localised tension in the gut. Clearly the self as a pure, thinking thing is inadequate to explain these sensations. Yet at the same time as our experience of Goya's work complicates the idea of a simple, transparent self, feelings of ambivalence or tension involved in our reactions seem to testify to some kind of unification between the multiplicity of interpretations the work generates; while understanding our responses often involves a connection with our past experiences. Such a self, which does experience continuity across time and interactions between divergent and complex feelings, is part of how we understand and describe our experiences and is the basis on which we make plans and engage in projects.

In this chapter, I will explore how in different ways the work of Nietzsche, Freud and Foucault challenges an idea of the self derived from Descartes's cogito, which reduces the self to a pure thinking thing. These thinkers do not simply deconstruct and problematise the self, however, but also offer resources to understand how a self that is not given can emerge. I will show how their work offers insights into the processes that contribute to the construction or forming of a self. We will see how self-construction, requiring unification of multiple elements, involves interpretation and is thus best characterised, following Foucault, as a hermeneutics of the self. Though I will argue in the course of this book that a hermeneutics of the self must be understood beyond the terms of textual hermeneutics; a task which non-literary artworks and artistic practice can help us undertake.

I will begin by considering how, with their different accounts of drives and their relation to an emergent self, Freud and Nietzsche can address the complexity and multiplicity of our encounter with artworks. In both thinkers, the development of these many drives, and of the production of a self from out of this multiplicity, is understood as an historical *process*. Given that the view of the self they propose is not of an unchanging thing, but of a material process, the process, or processes, can follow different paths, or vicissitudes in Freud's terms, suggesting the possibility of working on or altering the self, and of selves as we know them taking different forms.

I will go on to consider how Foucault adds to this account an analysis of the operation of power relations, in which the construction of a particular kind of subject or self itself forms a crucial part of the operation of power. Thus, the deconstruction and reconstruction of the self is a site of potential resistance to the structures of power. If we hope to take control of processes of self-construction, because we want to strengthen or work on aspects of ourselves, or to more radically transform ourselves,[1] then we need to understand the processes in which the self is established. We must, therefore, first address the problem of how the ongoing processes of construction, or interpretation, of the self act to cover themselves over, which is explored in different ways by these three thinkers. But we must also consider the problems these processes of disguise present for self-understanding, usefully articulated by Ricoeur in his discussion of the hermeneutics of suspicion.

In considering these different thinkers in relation to their views of the self, I wish to arrive at a description of the parameters of being a self that can navigate the tension between the complexity and mutability of our feelings and reactions, and our interpretation of them as the feelings of a particular self. The problematic of the self as something complex and emergent that we arrive at by drawing on the insights, and addressing the weaknesses of, Nietzsche, Freud and Foucault is one which raises the central question running through this book, namely how is a self which can incorporate multiple elements and processes constructed? I also hope to show that the lack of consensus concerning what is required to constitute a self and what forms of selfhood are possible or desirable leaves open the issue of exactly what counts as a self and what form the self could and should take. This suggests an important role for artworks in exploring how material process can give rise to different forms, as well as disrupt existing forms, and in contributing to experimentations in selfhood.

MULTIPLICITY

One of the strongest voices among the critics of the idea of a simple, given self is that of Friedrich Nietzsche. Nietzsche rejects the idea of a Cartesian self as an illusion: 'We have a phantom of "I" in mind [. . .] we want to create unity' by creating the illusion of a self as a single, conscious, continuous agency (Nietzsche 1988: vol. 8). We are invested in the idea of a unitary 'I' that thinks and decides and acts. This is the 'I' at the centre of our moral system, a self that we can praise and blame, and hold to account for past actions and future promises.

This account of the self is challenged by experiences of our own complexity. For Nietzsche, the competing experiences within us, such as the pity and sadistic enjoyment that the same person can feel for Goya's victims of war, or the relief and fear that we encounter in regard to ourselves in the face of these images, can be explained in terms of a multiplicity of drives: 'Our waking life is an interpretation of inner drive processes' (Nietzsche 1988: vol. 9, 216). It is worth pausing here to consider the meaning of interpretation. We normally understand interpretation through the model of the text, asking what the meaning expressed by the words is. On Nietzsche's understanding interpretation is not limited to the conscious ascription of meaning to text. Interpretation is involved in all our responses to stimuli, even at the level of seeing the world in terms of individuated objects. There is already active interpretation in having experiences, and there is further interpretation in the ascription of meaning, values and impetus to actions. For example, we, or rather for Nietzsche drives, interpret sensory information as an object, an object as an artwork, an artwork as good or bad. These interpretations can be explicit, writing a paper on the meaning of painting for example, but are also implicit in the actions we take, resting our gaze on this painting, handing over money to buy it, etc.

Nietzsche suggests that there are multiple drives offering different, often competing, sometimes collaborative interpretations. Hence, 'our' reactions to Goya's images are multiple and changeable because what is reacting is multiple and changeable. These drive processes involve tensions, 'our drives oftentimes contradict themselves' (Nietzsche 1988: vol. 9, 253), and shifting relations between drives and patterns of dominance, 'we always perceive the outer-world differently, because it is each time silhouetted against the dominant drive within us' (Nietzsche 1988: vol. 9, 209). Thus, Nietzsche's idea of a multiplicity of drives can explain both our feeling many different things in, for example, looking at an artwork at any given time, and how the experience, and the dominant interpretation of an artwork, changes between different encounters with the same work, as alliances and hierarchies of drives change.

The German term for drive, *Treib*, is derived from the verb *treiben*, to push. The drives push us to act and think, but also push towards their own expansion and development. Nietzsche ultimately understands the multiplicity of drives as a multiplicity of wills to power. He argues that: 'Our intellect, our will, likewise our feelings [*Empfindungen*] depend on our drives and the conditions of their existence. Our drives can be reduced to the will to power' (Nietzsche 1988: vol. 11, 661). Thus, we can understand *'man as a multiplicity of "wills to power": each one with a multiplicity of means of expression and forms'* (Nietzsche 1988: vol. 12, 25). Nietzsche's intention here is not to try to reduce all our motivations to a lust for power. Clearly, we are moved by many other desires and impulses, such as hunger and curiosity. The claim is not that what a drive to curiosity really means is a drive to power, but rather that we can best explain the emergence and operation of a drive to, for example, curiosity in terms of will to power. And thus, we can understand our thoughts, motivations and feelings in terms of will to power. But what does this mean? Nietzsche describes 'the essence of life, its *will to power*' in terms of 'spontaneous, aggressive, expansive, re-interpreting, re-directing and formative forces' (Nietzsche 2007: 52). Hence, the various drives characterised as wills to power are understood to always assert themselves in their difference. Our drives constantly develop and grow, overpowering, incorporating and shaping each other.[2]

This multiplicity of drives, understood in terms of will to power, features in Nietzsche's explanations of human psychology, anthropology and culture, and it is also these explanations, insofar as they are elucidating, that serve as evidence for the presence and character of these same drives or wills to power. We can understand the notion of drives that push us to act through commonly used examples such as a drive to sex or a drive to satisfy hunger. For Nietzsche, however, the notion of drives is much broader. Particular drives can come into existence in the context of society and culture. They can thus be understood to be shaped and to operate both within and beyond any individual, in interaction with other drives.

For instance, the drive to truth is a drive that has come into existence as part of the process of civilisation. Originally shaped by the needs of other drives it has come to be an important force pushing us towards certain behaviours and beliefs. Nietzsche begins his account of the emergence and development of the drive to truth, which he develops as a central theme throughout his philosophy, in his early essay *On Truth and Lying in a Nonmoral Sense* (1999). Here, truth emerges as a function of language and the communal concepts it employs. It involves overlooking the infinite variety in the world and makes generalisations so that we can make claims such as 'nightshade berries are poisonous' and 'apples are good to eat'. At this point, truth is not a critical examination of concepts but rather the creation and consolidation of concepts: 'that which is to count as "truth" from this point onwards now becomes fixed, i.e. a way of designating things is invented which has the same validity and force everywhere' (Nietzsche 1999: 143). As such, truth employs both creative drives and a drive to fix and make stable. It is a prerequisite for society and the benefits and protections that come with it. There are no pure motivations for Nietzsche; always at play are a complex set of drives and thus 'a whole host of the most various drives – curiosity, flight from boredom, envy, vanity, the desire for amusement, for example – can be involved in the striving for truth' (Nietzsche 1997: 89). Eventually, as Nietzsche chronicles in *Gay Science* 'knowledge and the striving for the true finally took their place as a need among the other needs. Henceforth, not only faith and conviction, but also scrutiny, denial, suspicion, and contradiction were a *power*' (Nietzsche 2001: 111). Though it is now a need, a drive, in itself, the drive to truth still operates in symbiosis with other drives. For example, when we destroy comforting beliefs by exposing them as illusions, a drive to cruelty finds expression through the operation of the drive to truth.

Nietzsche himself argues for an application of the will to power beyond an account of human characteristics, behaviour and beliefs (Nietzsche 2002: 36), but for my purposes I am concerned with how he uses it as an explanation of the complexity and tensions in our experiences, and ultimately of the material processes of self-construction. In this context, Nietzsche's account of multiple, competing forces of interpretation has explanatory force. Let us return to the example of Goya's prints. Say that I feel both compelled to look away and yet at the same time compelled to keep looking at a particular image, to keep turning the pages to see more, and to linger to take in the detail of images where the horror is not immediately apparent but emerges when you examine the scene. We can understand these experiences as the interpretation of different drives, competing against others as wills to power. A drive to avoid the pain aroused by empathy with the victims might push me towards averting my eyes from the image. The feelings these images arouse involve layers of interpretation; the interpretation that victims in the images are in pain, and that the pain induced in response to witnessing their pain is in some sense an injury, something to flee from. What then could keep me looking? Nietzsche would likely suggest as one contender the drive to truth, a need to know what Goya has depicted, what human beings are capable of. The drive to truth is interpreting the image as insightful, revelatory of human nature, bestowing of worthwhile knowledge. The drive to truth does not exist as an innate or fixed drive, however; as discussed above, its importance is one that has developed in our shared social history. And this development involved alliances with other drives. In compelling me to look at the images the drive to truth now operates in alliance with a drive to cruelty, which is seeking expression where it can, having been forced in the context of civilisation to turn inwards (Nietzsche 2007: 57). The drive to cruelty interprets the image as pleasurable. Thus, in Nietzsche's account we find both a tool for understanding our experiences and a means of understanding how the multiple forces that direct our interpretations and actions take shape in interrelation with each other at both an intra-

and inter-individual level. That Nietzsche's understanding of the formation and activity of drives operates both within and beyond individuals allows an integrated analysis of cultural and psychological phenomena, such as the drive to truth.

There is a risk in setting out, as Nietzsche does, to interpret all our experiences according to the hypothesis of will to power (Nietzsche 2002: 36); namely that we overlook other characteristics of drives that do not fit this guiding hypothesis. Further, Nietzsche's account of the interaction of drives operates at the level of the drives themselves, and not the individual (which is effectively a temporary alliance of drives on his account). Moreover, he models this interaction in terms of competition, though he is clear that this may involve symbiosis. Hence, elements of how individuals relate to each other, and the relevance of this to processes of *self*-construction, whether by oneself, by others, or by drives, may be neglected or distorted on Nietzsche's account. Nietzsche's theory of will to power offers a useful framework for understanding the interaction of a multiplicity of drives, and crucially how this involves interpretations and evaluations both at the level of the drives and the alliances they form. We can also learn from his recognition that these drives develop, and can be created, in social and cultural contexts, and are not contained within any one individual. But looking beyond Nietzsche can help us address potential gaps in his analysis and gain a more complete understanding of the multiple, interpretative processes that produce a self.

Another place that we find an account of the multiplicity to be found in responses to situations and objects, feelings, and explanations of behaviour in terms of the activity of a multiplicity of drives, is in the work of the founder of psychoanalysis, Sigmund Freud. Like Nietzsche, Freud explores both cultural and psychological phenomenon and sees a two-way interaction between internal drives and wider social practices and historical events. We shall see that what Freud adds to Nietzsche's analysis is a focus on the importance of concrete interactions between individuals, and in particular how our internal drives are partly shaped by the external objects, often significant others, that they attach to. Developing his understanding and treatment of psychological disorders in nineteenth-century Vienna, Freud moved in circles well acquainted with Nietzsche's work.[3] Despite protestations on Freud's part, the similarities in their account of human psychology and culture strongly suggest that the German philosopher did influence his thought, even if the differences between them are equally fundamental. Though translated as 'instinct' in the standard edition of his work, Freud most frequently employs not the German word *Instinkt*, but *Treib*, that for the most

part we find in Nietzsche and which is common to their shared heritage of German language philosophy and is more usually translated as
'drive'.[4]

Freud offers a dualistic account of our drives. He originally posited a
division between the libidinal drives and the drives of self-preservation
and later moved to the opposition of the libidinal drives, now encompassing self-preservation as a form of self-love, with the death drives,
which tend towards the removal of all excitation:

> Our views have from the very first been *dualistic*, and today they are even
> more definitely dualistic than before – now that we describe the opposition
> as being, not between ego drives and sexual drives, but between life drives
> and death drives. (Freud 2001: vol. XVIII, 53)

Within this dualism, however, which explains the inner conflict on
which Freud's account of our psychology depends (Wollheim 1991:
179), we can differentiate many drives. 'What distinguishes the drives
from one another and endows them with specific qualities is their
relation to their somatic sources and to their aims' (Freud 2001: vol.
VII, 168). Somatic sources are physical excitations within the body of
an organism. The general aim of all drives, according to Freud, is to
relieve this excitation. Different specific aims, however, will be required
to achieve this. For example, the oral drive has the aim of sucking
(Laplanche and Pontalis 1973: 22). The child 'proceeds to find this
satisfaction by sucking rhythmically at some part of the skin or mucous
membrane' (Freud 2001: vol. VII, 181). Drives are further differenti-
ated in relation to the objects they attach to and the particular history
of attachments that occur in a given individual.

Thus, in Freud we have a very different account of the drives from
that in Nietzsche, with drives originating from within a clearly defined
organism in contrast to Nietzsche's more open account of fluid boundaries that form a particular alliance of drives, in which drives or wills to
power can be seen to extend beyond a particular self. However, they
share an understanding that when we explain things at the level of a
self, many different drives are in operation.

What Freud adds to Nietzsche's account is his understanding of how
certain drives, the libidinal drives on his account, are object related.
We cannot understand the character, or interpretations, of such drives
without reference to their objects. This allows us to understand how
the relationships we form, and the actions of those we are in relationships with, influence the activity of the drives, including processes of
self-formation. The task of understanding, working on and shaping
ourselves does not occur in isolation. While Nietzsche is very aware

that we have been shaped in a social context, hence his belief that we need to escape this context if we are to change (Nietzsche 2007: 56–8), he fails to explore the inter-personal, relational operation of drives. Freud's work can, therefore, act as a useful corrective, drawing our attention to this aspect of drive behaviour (and, as I will discuss below, drive formation).

Freud's account of multiplicity is not limited to the drives themselves. In his late work he offers an account of psychical apparatus, based on the activity of the drives, that further divides the psychical into the processes of the id, the ego and the super-ego. In his account of these different systems Freud assigns the energy of the unconscious drives, the unknown forces that influence us, to the id, though not all that is unconscious can be identified with it (Freud 2001: vol. XIX, 23). The ego [*Ich*], which has 'a tendency to unity' (Freud 2001: vol. XIX, 45), emerges from the id as 'a coherent organization of mental processes' (Freud 2001: vol. XIX, 17). It is 'that part of the id which has been modified by the direct influence of the external world' (Freud 2001: vol. XIX, 25). It is to the ego, on Freud's account, that we owe our sense of self as distinct from the external world and it is the ego which consciously reflects and decides on courses of action. Freud compares the ego to the rider of a powerful horse: it modifies the demands of the id in the face of the environment, but often steers where the id wants to go anyway 'transforming the id's will into action as if it were its own' (Freud 2001: vol. XIX, 25). The third system, the super-ego is a critical and moral voice within us, an internalised parent that judges and watches (Freud 2001: vol. XIX, 36).

Freud's account thus rejects the idea of the self as a single agency which is able to fully determine a course of action or to impose one coherent interpretation. Something like Freud's ego or *Ich* is central to our experience, which involves a capacity to reflect on ourselves and thus be aware of ourselves as selves, and thus includes a capacity to distinguish ourselves from the wider world; capacities which Freud attributes to the ego. The self should not be reduced to the ego, however, as the drives that Freud locates in the id, and the structure of the super-ego, shape the experiences and actions of a self, by framing our interpretations and impelling us to act. If I enter into psychoanalytic treatment then the structures and agencies at work in addition to the ego are included in the meaning I give to my dreams, symptoms, interactions and behaviour. Thus, they cannot be excluded from my account of myself. These different processes are incorporated into my self-interpretation. At the same time as undermining the idea of a simple or transparent self, and fundamentally complicating any account of agency, Freud's understanding of distinct mental processes can be interpreted as forming a contingent, and tenuous, unity at the level of interpretation.

The tri-part division of the mind's system allowed Freud to tell a story about the symptoms of neurosis which he encountered in his medical practice. However the case studies are susceptible to multiple explanations, and Freud is perhaps guilty of overstepping the evidence due to the creativity of his own interpretations.[5] Thus, highlighting a fundamental problem of how we interpret the evidence for the activity of a complex and constructed self that is not, as the Cartesian 'thinking thing' is, transparent to introspection. This is a problem that I will return to below in the context of the methodological issues faced by a hermeneutics of the self that is also a hermeneutics of suspicion.

What we can take from both Nietzsche and Freud is that by recognising the multiplicity at play in the experiences and actions that we interpret as belonging to a particular self, we can more effectively acknowledge and explain the breadth and complexity of these experiences. Once we pay attention to this multiplicity, once we listen to and feel the activity of many drives, then any idea of the self as simple or as a pure mind or spirit that is disconnected from the body is shown to be inadequate. As Nietzsche says, 'pure spirit [*Geist*] is a pure lie' (Nietzsche 2005a: 8). We do not need subscribe to Nietzsche's account that all drives are ultimately will to power, or Freud's dualistic characterisation of the drives, but the idea of drives is an illuminating way of configuring the multiplicity of different corporeal forces, which we feel and which shape and motivate us, capturing the idea of multiple forces that are distinct yet intertwined. Both Nietzsche and Freud also understand this multiplicity as active and interactive. The multiple elements shaping our experience are also shaping each other in an ongoing process, which is crucial to an understanding of self-construction and thus the self as open to change. It is to process, therefore, that I know turn.

PROCESS

We began by considering the tension between the experience of multiplicity and what Freud would call the 'tendency to unity' which produces a self (Freud 2001: vol. XIX, 45). While in the example of looking at the Goya prints we are confronted with a complex array of feelings, we still experience them as *my* feelings. In both Nietzsche and Freud, we can understand the multiple, sometimes conflicting, feelings as the operation of drives. The self is then understood as emerging from the processes of these drives and their interactions. The understanding of the self, not as given but as continually produced, contrasts to 'the Cartesian question: Who am I?, as a unique but universal and unhistorical subject?' (Foucault 1982: 785). It also gives rise to the questions: how has my (individual and collective) history made possible the emergence of a self, how has it shaped the particular self I currently am, and how could this still be shaped and reshaped?

This historical, and mutable, character of the self can be understood firstly at the level of the drives. In addition to the multiplicity of the drives which Nietzsche describes as involved in the emergence of the drive to truth, we saw that he describes the drive to truth as developing gradually. Nietzsche claims that it is only after a long history in which 'every kind of drive took part in the fight about the "truths"' that a need for truth establishes itself in its own right (Nietzsche 2001: 111).

The extent to which a drive can change is more open on Nietzsche's understanding than on Freud's, as drives are not tied to particular somatic sources as they are for Freud. Nonetheless, Freud also traces the many 'vicissitudes' of the drives (Freud 2001: vol. XIV, 123). Drives, on his account, can attach to different objects and can come to acquire new intermediate aims, which 'may be changed any number of times in the course of the vicissitudes which the drive undergoes during its existence' (Freud 2001: vol. XIV, 122–3). The history of drives is a complex tale in Freud, he suggests that they can undergo:

Reversal into opposite.
Turning round upon the subject's own self.
Repression.
Sublimation. (Freud 2001: vol. XIV, 126)

An example of when a drive undergoes a reversal into its opposite is the movement from sadism to masochism. In this instance, the intermediate aim turns from an active aim to hurt others to a passive aim of being hurt. This involves a different interpretation of stimuli and different actions.

For Freud, not only the drives but also the distinct systems, or processes, in which he posits the drives operate must be understood in the context of their historical development. Freud is clear that 'a unity comparable to the ego cannot exist in the individual from the start; the ego has to be developed' (Freud 2001: vol. XIV, 77). The ego 'is first and foremost a bodily ego' that gradually distinguishes itself from the external world (Freud 2001: vol. XIX, 36). The ego, according to Freud, becomes aware of a difference between internal and external perceptions, the latter being perceptions that we can remove or exclude, shutting our eyes, or withdrawing our hand for instance. In making this distinction the ego becomes aware of itself and emerges through this self-awareness (Wollheim 1991: 187). While the complex story of the super-ego's emergence is bound up with Freud's theory of the Oedipus complex, Freud's theory of sexual development involves the deep ambivalence of a child towards its parents, which he believes is rooted in desire and jealously. In its simplest form this is what Freud refers to as the 'positive Oedipus complex' of the male child (the case of girls is more complicated).[6] The first object of desire being the mother's breast, the little boy later comes to desire his mother and thus perceive the father as competition. In Freud's story, the murderous feelings that follow produce great anxiety, both for the father, who the boy loves, and for the boy himself, because he fears his father will discover his murderous wish and punish him in the form of castration. Hence, Freud appropriates the myth of Oedipus in which Oedipus unwittingly fulfils the prophecy that he will murder his father and marry his mother. The resolution of this complex involves 'either an identification with his mother or an intensification of his identification with his father' (Freud 2001: vol. XIX, 32). In fact, Freud hypothesises an element of bisexuality as universal, and suggests that both elements, and ambivalence towards both parents, exist to a certain extent in everyone. Freud claims these ambivalent feelings towards our parents – desire, fear and identification – lead to the formation of the ego ideal and super-ego (Freud 2001: vol. XIX, 34). If the ego ideal suggests the positive aspect of identification with the parent, providing a model that we aim to be like, the super-ego designates the punishing aspects of our internalised parents. Freud goes on to account for the intensity of the super-ego's judgements in the repression of the Oedipus complex and the injunction that we cannot be entirely like the parent we identify with because the love object they enjoy is prohibited to us. According to Freud, the super-ego borrows the strength from the father figure to effect this repression and dominates the ego 'in the form of conscience or perhaps of an unconscious sense of guilt' (Freud 2001: vol. XIX, 35).

Freud's analysis of the phenomenon of guilt in terms of the emergence of the super-ego is itself an interpretation. He offers a story that gives meaning to various behaviours, feelings and tensions. But what Freud's controversial account of the Oedipus complex provides is perhaps not so much a decisive case for the particular story he tells us, as evidence for our need to provide an interpretation in order to make sense of our experiences. Such interpretation and storytelling are part of the process of the hermeneutics of the self, which presents problems for self-knowledge that I will discuss in the next section of this chapter. Freud has not successfully demonstrated that his interpretation is the best interpretation in terms of its details. Where Freud most convinces is in suggesting that the character, and form of expression, of powerful, bodily drives is partly determined by their objects. This in turn implies that the objects which we, as a conglomeration of drives, desire partly determine us. Thus, if we are to understand processes of self-construction, we not only need to take account of the drives' interactions within a self but also with external objects including other selves. Our interactions with artworks provide an opportunity for exploring and playing with the activity of object-related drives.

In both Nietzsche and Freud, the activity of drives, which shape the self, can occur in the history of a particular self but also on a group level in our shared cultural histories. For example, on the level of the individual, Freud's understanding of neurotic symptoms, such as the obsessive repetition of rituals and personality disorders, rests on an account of deviation from normal sexual development (Freud 2001: vol. VII, 125–245). There are three key stages in his account. The first is fixation, in which a drive is prevented from becoming conscious and developing. Subsequently any associated ideas or thoughts are repressed. The third stage is that the repressed material returns and is expressed at the point of fixation. The nature of the neurotic symptom is determined by the stage of development (oral, anal, phallic or genital) at which fixation occurred in an individual's libidinal development, in interaction with their ego-development (Wollheim 1991: 150). Freud's story thus connects the neurotic compulsions in an adult and their particular experiences as an infant. But Freud's analysis is not limited to events that occur at an individual level but also takes in collective experiences. This is apparent in his account of guilt. Freud claims that civilisation requires that man's 'aggressiveness is introjected, internalized; it is, in point of fact, sent back to where it came from – that is, it is directed towards his own ego' (Freud 2001: vol. XXI, 123). The agent of aggression on Freud's analysis is the super-ego. We have seen that Freud accounts for the super-ego in terms of individual development in response to the universal experience of the Oedipus complex. He also, however, incorporates into his understanding of guilt the idea of significant historical events, suggesting that beyond the individual guilt we each feel for wishing to murder our father is the species guilt of an actual murder: 'men have always known (in this special way) that they once possessed a primal father and killed him' (Freud 2001: vol. XXIII, 101).

Freud's account of guilt echoes Nietzsche's earlier remarks on internalised aggression. While for Freud this is part of the problem of understanding both normal and pathological psychology, for Nietzsche it is part of his genealogical analysis of morality, which serves as a critique of Christian morality, aiming to destabilise our faith in it and open the space for a revaluation of values. In *On the Genealogy of Morality* (2007) Nietzsche accounts for how moral practices and the modern man we know today have emerged. Modern man is moral man – able to live in social groups, make and keep promises, and be held accountable for his actions. In addition to the invention of moral principles, this requires memory, and conscience so that these principles are enforced. Nietzsche asks not only how did we come to have a conscience, but how did it come to be so punishing towards us? In civilised society our aggressive drives cannot be allowed free expression. This 'had the result that those instincts of the wild, free, roving man were turned backwards, *against man himself*'. This is what Nietzsche's calls 'the *internalisation* of man'. Our interior self 'extended itself and gained depth, breadth and height in proportion to the degree that the external discharge of man's instincts was *obstructed*'. These internalised instincts include 'cruelty, the pleasure of pursuing, raiding, changing and destroying'. These cruel and aggressive instincts need an outlet. Hence, civilised man 'became the inventor of "bad conscience"' in order 'to create from within himself an adventure, a torture-chamber' (Nietzsche 2007: 57). Nietzsche recognises this process of constant development everywhere: 'the whole history of a "thing", an organ, a tradition can to this extent be a continuous chain of signs, continually revealing new interpretations and adaptations' (Nietzsche 2007: 51). For Nietzsche, the process of competition between the interpretations of our various wills to power, their incorporations, alliances and accompanying adaptations, ultimately explains the character of modern of man and the state of modern culture.

The above examples show that in both Nietzsche and Freud there is explanatory force in accounts that trace the vicissitudes of drives, that operate both within and beyond particular selves. The history of a drive is not an isolated process. A drive's development is always in interaction with other drives. As well as drives affecting each other, their interactions can create new drives and establish different alliances of drives. Understanding the development and activity of particular drives is crucial to understanding the development of particular selves. But equally our particular histories as selves, and the actions, interactions, attachments to objects and interpretations these histories encompass, are part of the history of our drives, and we cannot reduce the self to its component drives. Hence the processes that produce a self are multiple, complex and historical.

The differences in Nietzsche's and Freud's accounts, however, emphasise for us that the stories of a drive, an individual, a species that they offer are themselves interpretations. These competing interpretations may both elucidate our experiences and contribute to our self-construction, but they can also participate in certain patterns of distortion, favouring for instance, as Freud seems to, what can be linked to a shared language of symbol and myth and thus reinforcing this narrative. It is Michel Foucault who takes up the notion that our sense of self is formed in the context of power relations and adds to this an analysis of the power strategies of individuals, institutions and government. He offers concrete examples of how power is exercised in ways that shape a particular kind of subject: namely a self that is self-aware as an agent and subject to the operations of contemporary power.

To understand Foucault's analysis of the self as a product of power relations we must first clarify what he means by power. Power, according to Foucault, exists only in its exercise and 'is exercised from innumerable points, in the interplay of non-egalitarian and mobile relations' (Foucault 1978: 94). Foucault describes power as:

> a total structure of actions brought to bear upon possible actions; it incites, it induces, it seduces, it makes easier or more difficult; in the extreme it constrains or forbids absolutely; it is nevertheless always a way of acting upon an acting subject or acting subjects by virtue of their acting or being capable of action. (Foucault 1982: 789)

These actions – which are always reactions to the power strategies of others, a problem for self-determinacy which I shall return to in Chapter 4 – include those in which the self establishes itself as a particular kind of subject.

Foucault claims that a unifying theme in this work is an historical exploration of the 'different modes by which, in our culture human beings are made subjects' (1982: 208). One example of this is the account he offers in *Discipline and Punish* of how Jeremy Bentham's Panopticon contributes to the creation of a particular kind of self as a self-monitoring subject. This architectural prison design places a prisoner in a position where they cannot tell if they are being watched. They are aware that they are always potentially visible and therefore censor their own behaviour. Foucault argues that the Panopticon operates 'to induce in the inmate a state of conscious and permanent visibility that assures the automatic functioning of power' (Foucault 1995: 201). The architectural model is one that Foucault thinks extends into social structures. In a society that orders itself according to the Panoptic structure, a constant feeling of being monitored leads to our monitoring ourselves, and this creates an interiority as the object of self-observation. In his later work, Foucault becomes increasingly interested in what he terms 'governmentality', which is concerned with 'the technologies of domination of others and those of the self' (Foucault 1988: 19). Governmentality introduces the notion that we act not just to influence the conduct of others but to control our own conduct, and to control how others will control their own conduct. It thus employs various technologies of the self which:

> permit individuals to effect by their own means or with the help of others, a certain number of operations on their own bodies and souls, thoughts, conduct, and way of being, so as to transform themselves in order to attain a state of happiness, purity, wisdom, perfection or immortality. (Foucault 1988: 18)

In his final works, Foucault turns to these methods of working on the self as a possible means of resistance 'against that which ties the individual to himself and submits him to others in this way (struggles against subjection, against forms of subjectivity and submission)' (1982: 781). For Foucault, we are modern subjects insofar as we are tied to our identity through self-awareness. Our identity and our awareness of our identity is produced in the context of power relations, in response to the power tactics of others, and involves our subjugation (1982: 781). To question identity, and the forms of subjectivity available to us, loosening these ties and creating space for experiment and new identities, is thus a form of resistance to the power structures we operate within. I will take up the idea of our taking control of the processes in which our sense of self is formed as a form resistance in Chapters 4 and 5. We will see how, if the operations of power which shape and limit self-construction include visual representations and restrictions on bodily comportment, then we need visual and bodily responses in order to critique and go beyond a subjugated self.

So, we have seen how these diverse thinkers all suggest the importance of recognising multiple processes within the self and multiple processes and practices influencing the construction of the self. Nietzsche highlights the importance of the interactions between drives, Freud brings a new attention to the influence of particular relations with others, and Foucault to the role of the systems and practices that constitute a particular configuration of power relations. In each, tracing the history of a drive, a practice, a way of understanding ourselves as selves becomes crucial to understanding what is involved in the construction of a self, and to any possibility of cultivating or changing the shape this takes. And, on Foucault's analysis, to resisting operations of power and disrupting the current stratification of power relations. They all elaborate a view of selves as undergoing continual construction and interpretation, rather than as simply given, which makes possible projects of working on the self and even radical self-transformation.

Such projects depend on understanding the different levels on which this construction operates. All three thinkers that I have discussed offer accounts of self-construction as operating at multiple levels, within and beyond particular selves. They also all claim that the processes of self-construction work to cover themselves over. We need, therefore, to explore the forms of disguise Freud, Nietzsche and Foucault hypothesise, but also to consider the problem of deciphering these disguises.

A HERMENEUTICS OF SUSPICION

In developing their views on the nature of the self and self-construction, Nietzsche, Freud and Foucault all see themselves as challenging existing assumptions. For Nietzsche, to take an honest look at ourselves as individuals and a species could result in a potentially devastating blow to our self-esteem. This is inseparable from his analysis of our values and belief system, which form the preconditions of our actions and our interpretations of them. His genealogical investigation of the roots and legacy of the Christian worldview suggest that it is an embodiment of an Ascetic Ideal that has dominated Western society in various guises. This ideal is ascetic both because it is cruelly unobtainable and because it denigrates the this-worldly and bodily in favour of a transcendent, other-worldly goal; whether this is Plato's forms, the Christian God and afterlife, or scientific faith in an objective truth (Nietzsche 2005a: 171). Adherents of the Ascetic Ideal also advocate ascetic practices of self-denial that attempt to deny, restrict or punish bodily desires, such as a monk's celibacy, hair shirts and meagre diet. In this context, our sense of self-worth is bound up with the idea of ourselves as something higher than other animals, rational, and above the body and its desires. Nietzsche suggests that to challenge this is to challenge the 'gold-dust of unconscious human vanity' (Nietzsche 2002: 123). He lampoons the so-called 'objective men' and 'pure-perceivers', calling the latter 'lechers', 'cowards' and 'habitual liars' (Nietzsche 2002: 97, 2005b: 106–7).[7] His suggestion here is that these men are impure and dishonest in their denial of the bodily roots of their motivations and ideals. The attempt to control the drives itself emerges from the drives.

Where Nietzsche suggests we cannot face the activity of drives in general, and accept our corporeality, Freud suggests it is specific drives and the object-specific wishes they give rise to which we find unbearable. His story of the Oedipus complex, discussed above, is shocking, requiring as it does the claim of taboo libidinal investments in our parents. His particular interpretations of dreams suggest the presence of disguised wishes that are disguised precisely because they are at odds with what is considered socially and morally acceptable. These wishes find disguised expression in our dreams because they cannot find expression in reality due to the 'repugnance felt for the topic of the dream or for this wish derived from it' (Freud 2001: vol. 4, 160).

Hence, the problem of understanding the activity shaping us is deeper than a desire to avoid the cruelty and damage to our sense of self that honesty towards oneself could engender. The activity tends to hide itself precisely because it is unacceptable to, or painful for, us. To understand our self-construction, we therefore have to learn how to uncover it. According to Freud, opposing forces keep certain ideas from becoming conscious, thereby actively establishing and maintaining 'the dynamically unconscious repressed' (Freud 2001: vol. XIX, 14–15).[8] This is to be distinguished from what is unconscious merely in the sense of latent, or not currently being thought about, but capable of becoming conscious. Freud states:

> we have been obliged to assume – that very powerful mental ideas exist (and here a quantitative or *economic* factor comes into question for the first time) which can produce all the effects in mental life that ordinary ideas do (including effects that can in their turn become conscious as ideas), though they themselves do not become conscious. (Freud 2001: vol. XIX, 14)

It is in encountering resistance within the psychoanalytic practice that Freud maintains that the forces of repression are discovered. 'The resistance accompanies the treatment step by step' (Freud 2001: vol. XII, 103). The 'strongest weapon of resistance' is transference (Freud 2001: vol. XII, 104). Positive or negative feelings the patient, or 'analysand', develops towards the analyst in a psychoanalytic relationship, such as feelings of love for the analyst, can lead to distracting obsessions or sudden cessation in the therapy. But this resistance operates as a clue to the presence of the very forces that drive it. Psychoanalytic treatment aims to employ the transference, which Freud claimed makes accessible and active the repressed conflict in order to work through that conflict and affect a cure (Freud 2001: vol. XXIII, 231, vol. XVI, 436). The key point here, however, is that at the heart of the dynamic activity that shapes the Freudian self is the activity of repression, which is inherently obscured from our conscious awareness.

If we return to Nietzsche, we see wills to power operate in a way that tends to obscure their character as wills to power. Nietzsche's aim in his employment of genealogy is to reveal the historical development of concepts and ideas that are presented as given, and to show the complexity of their origins and the stages they have gone through. The success of a given concept may depend precisely on denying its character as an *interpretation* and thus its history as a will to power that has established, moulded and pushed this interpretation. For Nietzsche 'it is altogether impossible to *live* at all without forgetting' (Nietzsche 1997: 62). This includes the ability to forget the invention of an ideal as a prerequisite for that ideal to function. If Christianity was established to protect us from the devastating effects of nihilism in the face of our impotence and suffering, it can only work if we forgot this and believe in the story of an afterlife that it offers us (Ansell-Pearson and Large 2006: 383). The success of the Christian interpretation thus depends on our ignorance of its history. Hence, for Nietzsche that which 'wants to dominate itself and its surroundings, and to feel its domination', i.e. will to power, tends to 'incorporate new "experiences," to classify new things into old classes, – which is to say: it aims at growth, or, more particularly the *feeling* of growth' but is also 'served by an apparently opposite drive of spirit, a suddenly emerging resolution in favour of ignorance and arbitrary termination' and has both an 'occasional will to be deceived' and a 'willingness to deceive others' (2002: 122). Nietzsche suggests that: 'What the spirit enjoys here is its multiplicity of masks and its artfulness, and it also enjoys the feeling of security these provide, – after all, its Protean arts are the very things that protect and conceal it the best!' (2002: 122).

This effectiveness of disguise as a tactic is clear in Foucault's analysis of power. The most successful operation of power may be one in which we are unaware of the operation of power. For Foucault, power is omnipresent and inescapable. It is not possessed but exercised from multiple points, and it does not operate primarily in terms of prohibition or repression but in a 'productive role' (Foucault 1978: 94), including the production of a particular kind of subject. This is to be contrasted with a simplistic, top-down view of power as operating primarily through prohibition and censorship. In the context of his discussion on the deployment of sexuality within power strategies, Foucault suggests that a view of power as repression is:

> Defined in a strangely restrictive way, in that, to begin with this power is poor in resources, sparing of its methods, monotonous in the tactics it utilizes, incapable of invention, and seemingly doomed always to repeat itself. Further, it is a power that only has the force of the negative on its side, a power to say no; in no condition to produce, capable only of positing limits, it is basically anti-energy. This is the paradox of its effectiveness: it is incapable of doing anything, except to render what it dominates incapable of doing anything either. (Foucault 1978: 85)

Why then is the view of power as repression so prevalent and 'what explains this tendency not to recognize' the operation of subtle and various forms of power? The answer Foucault suggests is that 'power is tolerable only on condition that it mask a substantial part of itself. Its success is proportional to its ability to hide its own mechanisms' (Foucault 1978: 86).

If Foucault is right that power tends to mask itself, and that the formation of the self is itself part of the operation of power tactics, then the formation of the contemporary self tends to mask itself. Essential to his project of uncovering the various modes in which a self-aware and self-monitoring subject is formed is an analysis of the interaction between techniques of domination, in which we impose aims on others, and technologies of the self, in which 'individuals effect, by their own means, a certain number of operations on their own bodies, on their own souls, on their own thoughts, on their own conduct' (Foucault 1993: 204). Within this interaction, the way in which we talk about ourselves – which for Foucault produces what we take to be the truth about ourselves – is central, and thus practices of confession, whether in the context of Christianity, literature, or medicine and psychotherapy, operate to produce a particular self. Foucault describes how in Christianity we have a duty to know ourselves, not just our actions but our thoughts and temptations, and bear witness against ourselves (1993: 211). The demand to confess, extending beyond the context of Christianity and into medical, juridical and educational contexts, and to admit to our 'true' sexual nature and hidden desires, is used to secure our participation in processes of examination, observation and documentation (Foucault 1978: 53–73). Thus, we take up the practices that shape us into self-examining and self-policing subjects without being aware of this.

So, in addition to acknowledging the historicity of the self, and thus the need to explore the history of how we have emerged as selves if we are to understand, and possibly change, ourselves, Nietzsche, Freud and Foucault also share the view that this history is partially obscured. To tell the history of the production of the self requires that we uncover or decipher this history, to the extent that this is possible. This presents a problem of interpretation.

This is clear in the example of Freud's interpretation of dreams, which he argues gives access to the repressed material of the unconscious and is thus crucial to self-knowledge. Here the manifest content of the dream is distinguished from its latent content: its real meaning as wish fulfilment. The forces of repression only allow the repressed wishes to express themselves in disguised form. The 'dream-work' condenses, displaces and represents the wish. Condensation omits some elements and layers others to express the latent content in an abbreviated form.

Displacement means that the latent content is expressed through an allusion, by for instance something that is associated with the real object of concern. Hence what is important to the dream's meaning may be a trivial element of the manifest content, a minor character or event not central to the dream's 'plot'. Finally, representation allows dreams to be translated into visual images, or symbols. The dream thus stands in need of interpretation by the analyst to reach its latent content and unveil its meaning (Freud 2001: vol. XV, 170–83).

Ricoeur suggests that this is to move from an understanding of the symbol as analogy to one in which we have to investigate a 'multitude of ruses and falsifications of meaning' (1970: 17). Ricoeur groups Nietzsche and Freud with Marx as the masters of 'the school of suspicion' (1970: 32). 'Beginning with them, understanding is hermeneutics: henceforward, to seek meaning is no longer to spell out the consciousness of meaning, but to *decipher its expressions*' (Ricoeur 1970: 33). And this in turn requires 'the invention of an art of *interpreting*' (Ricoeur 1970: 33).

This need for interpretation or decoding presents methodological problems. Firstly, if we have no access to the way things are prior to or beneath the process of disguise, whether this is conceived of as repression or as the cunning of power, how do we ever know that we have the right interpretation? Put bluntly – we do not. There is no truth behind interpretation or a single correct interpretation that we can finally arrive at. There is only a process of exposing these processes of disguise through critical analysis, making better sense of our experiences and putting into practice our insights with the spirit of experiment. For example, Nietzsche would suggest that once we reveal the operation of partial drives at the heart of an ideal that presents itself as absolute and transcendent, then we can no longer naively accept this self-presentation. Further, the account of will to power that has operated as Nietzsche's principle of critique has positive explanatory force. In terms of European history, it explains the success of Christianity. At a personal level, it also explains the complexity of our experiences, as in our encounter with Goya's prints. In psychoanalysis, evidence that its interpretation supersedes our conscious knowledge prior to the analytic encounter is offered in the cure of neurosis, or at least patients feeling happier and breaking patterns of behaviour, because they have come to a *better* interpretation of their own behaviour in relation to their own past, even if we cannot claim it is the last or only interpretation.

The fundamental problem is that various different interpretations seem to make good sense of our experiences and can provide useful tools for us. What makes one interpretation better than another? I would suggest that a better interpretation is understood in terms of the method or art of interpretation. When Nietzsche writes of 'bad arts of interpretation' it is in the context of suggesting that the idea of natural law comes from a 'polite ulterior motive' that falsely treats nature as fact or text (2002: 22). From Nietzsche's perspective, a better art of interpretation is one that has the honesty of acknowledging that it is an interpretation. There is no final text behind the activity of interpretation. And there are various factors, ultimately various drives and wills to powers, at work in shaping our interpretation. A better art of interpretation requires us to be more aware of the factors which drive our interpretations, mitigating their influence even as we seek to discern their operation.

Nietzsche, Freud and Foucault would all take themselves to be finding evidence for their hypothesis of the process of disguise in the decoding of material that they provide. There is always the danger, however, that if we approach phenomena, whether the practices of a major religion or an individual's dream, with a hypothesis, such as will to power, or the repressed Oedipus complex, that hypothesis may tend to be confirmed because we incorporate what fits into our story and are blind to what does not. Thus, it is important that we maintain a constant awareness that the assumptions employed in a practice of interpretation are assumptions that are open to revision. Artworks can have a role to play in provoking alternative and competing interpretations. They can allow us in Nietzschean terms to inhabit and move between different interpreting perspectives. We also need to learn to pay attention to the liminal and the apparently insignificant, rather than focusing only on dominant cultural themes.

The function of power may work against this much needed openness and modesty in our interpretive arts. The operation of power presents a further methodological problem for hermeneutics. To believe one has found evidence for one's own interpretation is also to justify one's own supposed expertise and practices, and thus entrench one's power. The psychoanalyst justifies the psychoanalytic practice when they reveal to you a repressed complex. Foucault is highly aware of this and posits that even the idea that there is something to decode – in particular in the context of the history of sexuality that there is a 'hidden' or 'repressed' sexual identity or desire – plays its part within power strategies, with the 'obligation to draw out' the truth of sex in which we are 'dedicated to the endless task of forcing its secret' (Foucault 1978: 159). Thus, as part of our art of interpretation, we must be suspicious against any 'masters' of suspicion and capable of unpacking how their own bias may operate as a further complication in the masking processes.

An example of this self-suspicion within psychoanalytic practice is the demand for awareness of the existence of counter-transference, in which the analyst transfers feelings from their own drive conflicts onto the patient. As a discipline with many developments and versions we also see criticisms from within psychoanalytic theory of Freud's particular interpretations and tendency to generalise interpretations.

Crucially, we need to avoid the trap that Foucault points to of thinking we are simply uncovering a 'hidden' or true self. There is no final interpretation of the self not only because there is no access to unmediated truth generally, but because the process of interpreting or knowing the self is part of the production of that self. There is no text of the self to interpret. Deciphering the processes of self-construction is itself part of that construction. Thus, attempting to interpret various aspects of the self, from dreams, to relationships, to self-presentation, is always a process that not only works towards self-understanding but also produces the self it attempts to understand.

Hence, Foucault's term of a 'hermeneutics of the self' (Foucault 1993). Self-construction is an interpretative activity. This interpretation is multiple and occurring on different levels and in the weaving together of these different levels. We have seen that, if Nietzsche and Freud are right, these interpretations are ultimately those of bodily drives. But they also involve the technologies and practices these drives produce, and which will in turn affect these drives. Foucault elaborates the cultural and institutional activities that contribute to a hermeneutics of the self. But this hermeneutics always works on and through the body. Foucault provides us with concrete examples of how the body is modified through various technologies of the self. While we cannot ever access a body free from cultural interpretation, the body is ineliminable and the practices that produce a self explored by Foucault include those that work on the body. Thus, interpretation is somatic. This claim is supported by paying attention to the sensations involved in an encounter with artworks. And it is this which I will argue narrative theories of the self elide, and an appeal to visual art will help us explore. Ultimately, the claim that narrative theory fails as an account of self-construction because it excludes numerous corporeal processes will be supported by showing, with the support of visual art, the corporeality of various processes of self-construction that cannot be incorporated by narrative theory.

UNIFYING PRINCIPLES

If the self is a product of a hermeneutics of the self, and the various drive interpretations and practices it encompasses, then the question of hermeneutic method cannot be reduced to an epistemological one concerning the problems inherent in any art of interpretation, but is also normative: what are the principles or goals that drive and direct this process of self-construction? What degree and form of unity is adequate, and desirable for a self? And who decides these criteria of selfhood?

In Freud, the norm of health operates as a basis for the practice of psychoanalysis to offer a cure to the neurotic. The gradual emergence of the ego system is essential to the emergence of a self-aware, unified ego (Freud 2001: vol. XIX, 45; vol. XIV, 77). For Freud, a healthy self requires a strong ego. An excessively strong super-ego or an ego that is damaged through its own mechanisms of defence, for instance splitting itself, are counter to healthy development (Wollheim 1991: 202–3). Freud is thus operating with an ideal of mental health in which his practice of working on the self aims to address the problems of abnormal development, and thus remove anxiety and neurotic behaviour, such as a phobia, caused by the repressed psychical conflict. He does not propose a radical reconfiguration of the self.

However, a hermeneutics of the self may have more radical goals than conforming with a conventional notion of health and allowing an individual to fit into a socially acceptable role. The notion of what form of self, or kind of unity, should be aimed at, or even what the minimal requirements to constitute a self are, need not be assumed in advance but can be open to experimentation.

In a key passage from *The Gay Science* Nietzsche speaks of style as a constraint and claims that:

> *One thing is needful.* – To 'give style' to one's character – a great and rare art! It is practiced by those who survey all the strengths and weaknesses that their nature has to offer and then fit them into an artistic plan. (2001: 163)

There is no one template of what counts as a successful stylistic unity of character. Indeed, if it is a question of incorporating the distinctive combination of drives available to each of us it requires many different, individual iterations. Art presents itself as an obvious model for exploring what this notion of style as a guiding principle of unification could involve, and also emphasises the plurality of possibilities. In fact, the idea of literary style has been proposed as one way of understanding giving style to one's self in Nietzsche himself (Nehamas 1985: 8).

It may be that an individual's practices for working on – and thus I argue the means of producing – the self require goals to give them content. For example, the Stoic's practice of envisaging challenges or future difficulties is aimed at their goal of self-reliance. The goal of simply producing a self rather than cultivating a strong self, or a happy self, or an artistically pleasing self, seems empty. To understand the various processes that produce a self includes an account of their various aims, and an interpretation of why becoming a certain kind of self, or a self at all, is valuable. For example, practices of self-examination can be understood in terms of an alliance between a drive to truth and a Stoic concern for self-control. But the goals of our drives, and drive alliances, can be, as Nietzsche suggests, particular to the individual rather than following an established or universal template. And further, as Freud elaborated, the aims of our drives will be shaped by our interactions with others and objects they attach to. Thus, while an analysis of processes of self-formation may require an account of the aims of these processes, there does not need to be a universal teleology.

Foucault's hope is that whatever the particular goals or type of self we might aim at, we can find ways to employ technologies of the self that can avoid the production of a subjugated subject. Despite always operating in the context of power relations Foucault suggests there is the space for creative responses to the strategies of others (Foucault 1982: 790). Artworks again provide an important model for how novelty, and the disruption of existing hierarchies, can be created with existing materials and from within the context that it disrupts. Art has been able to ask the question of what art is from within the art world, pushing at its own boundaries. When for example Marcel Duchamp places a ready-made urinal in an art gallery (*Fountain*, 1917), the possibilities for what can count as an artwork are expanded.

What is clear from the theories we have surveyed in this chapter is that there is a lack of consensus concerning what constitutes adequate unity between various drives, drive alliances and practices, to produce a self or what form this should take. In this book, I do not want to assume one model of what a self can be, and what it is desirable for a self to be. We can usefully take from Freud his understanding of the other related nature of drives, as an important corrective to Nietzsche, and the importance of sexuality to which his corpus so powerfully draws attention, without adhering to his prescriptive account of what a healthy self should constitute. With Nietzsche and Foucault we can remain open as to what form the self can take. This openness lies at the intersection of a hermeneutics as a method of understanding our experiences and a hermeneutics as a method of creating (if only temporarily) adequate unity among disparate elements to operate as a self. We should neither assume that there is a true self to reveal nor a template that the self that emerges must conform to.

What then is required is investigation and experimentation in different forms of becoming a self. Artworks again provide us with a model. What can count as an artwork, and what makes a successful artwork, is an open question in creative activity that parallels the openness that is required in a hermeneutics of the self. Particular artworks also provide us with profound examples that address different identities and configurations of the self, such as Louise Bourgeois's explorations of motherhood and Cindy Sherman's play with representations of women.

CONCLUSION

What this discussion has shown us is that Nietzsche, Freud and Foucault, in order to do justice to the multiplicity and mutability of experiences, all move away from an account of the self as given, to a process view of the self. Further, they all understand the multiple processes operating within and creating the self as ultimately corporeal. In Freud and Nietzsche this is explicit in their view of self as shaped by multiple, interacting bodily drives. The self may be created through an interpretation, but ultimately it is the drives which interpret. For Foucault too the various practices and technologies by which we affect changes on selves, both others and ourselves, include those that act on and through the body. The move to a view of the self as constructed through various interpretative, ultimately corporeal, processes both opens the possibility of changing the kind of self we are and problematises how we can become a self at all. We establish, and continually re-establish, the self, making possible our projects and self-understanding as actors, and we do this in particular contexts and through particular processes. This hermeneutics of the self involves interactions at different levels: between the drives within us, between different developing selves, and between different collectives. It incorporates the interpretations of our drives and social and cultural interpretations and involves a range of practices, beliefs and actions.

One way that various philosophers, including Ricoeur, have attempted to understand how unity could be created and sustained from out of the ongoing multi-level and multi-directional activity occurring, is through the model of literature, and in particular novels and stories. This model treats the hermeneutics of the self as analogous to the production and reading of a written text and borrows the structure of narrative from the world of literature. In the next chapter, I will explore the power but also the limitations of the narrative model of self-construction by focusing on the narrative model developed by Ricoeur. We will see that these limitations indicate the need to find an alternative model for a hermeneutics of the self in the work of non-literary artists which more effectively recognises the corporeality of processes of self-construction and understands interpretation more broadly than a textual analogy permits.

NOTES

1. As discussed in the Introduction if, as Foucault argues, the form of self that is produced is produced in the context of power relations then resistance to these power relations may involve the disruption of these forms of being a self. Nietzsche's philosophy also contains an argument for why we should aim at such radical transformation; his analysis of the problem of nihilism connects it to the kind of being the human has become, and the possibility of overcoming of nihilism requires an overcoming of the human in some sense (2005b: 250). Nietzsche asks what *'could be bred from humanity'* (2002: 92), which in turn requires experiments in living at the level of the individual (2002: 91; also 1986: 5–11).

2. For detailed discussions of Nietzsche's will to power see Heidegger (1991), Mitcheson (2013), Moore (2002), Müller-Lauter (1999), Poellner (1995) and Richardson (1996).

3. Ronald Lehrer chronicles Freud's correspondence with friends who knew Nietzsche's work, as well as his exposure to Nietzsche's ideas via talks at the Vienna Psychoanalytic Society, and likely reading of some of Nietzsche's texts, despite Freud seeming to claim the contrary (Lehrer 1995).

4. I have changed the translation of *Treib*, as opposed to *Instinkt*, to 'drive' rather than instinct when quoting from the standard edition of Freud's works.

5. For example, the case of the Little Hans, which Freud based on observations recorded in letters by Hans's father, has been revisited with alternative interpretations offered by Melanie Klein, John Bowlby and Jacques Lacan, who all offer different explanations for Hans's phobia of horses (Midgley 2006).

6. Freud struggled to answer the question of how it is that girls come to give up the mother as a love object in favour of the father. In a paper of 1925, he came to formulate a much criticised theory (by for instance Karen Horney and Melanie Klein) in which penis envy plays a key role, the mother being blamed for this lack, and desire for a penis being replaced by desire for a child, the girl's love object then becoming the father (Freud 2001: vol. XIX, 248–58). Luce Irigaray summarises objections to the problems in Freud's approach to understanding the development of female sexuality in her essay 'Psychoanalytic Theory: Another Look'. Irigaray suggests that Freud's approach is premised on a view of the pre-Oedipal stage in which the girl's desire for her mother is a *masculine* desire, and the little girl is reduced to a little man with a truncated penis for genitals, failing to recognise any genuinely *female* sexuality (Irigaray 1985: 34–67).

7. In this passage from *Thus Spoke Zarathustra* (2005) Nietzsche is alluding

to Plato's discussion of the lover of sights in *The Republic* (Plato 1997: 1102) and reversing Plato's criticisms of them, claiming that it is the deniers of the senses who are impure. For Nietzsche, the Ascetic Ideal can be connected to the claim in *The Republic* that the senses detract from the pursuit of truth, which is also the pursuit of virtue or value.

8. The problem of the forces of repression can be understood from three perspectives. From the topographical perspective, Freud's division of the psychical into different sub-systems or functions, repression is carried out by the ego as a form of defence. From the economic perspective, by which we mean the question of the energy the ego has to harness for these forces to succeed, there is a complex interaction of investments or cathexes [*Bezetung*], accumulations of psychical energy when it attaches to particular drives, ideas or objects. Finally, there is the question of the motive, or the dynamic point of view, which is the intense pain that awareness of these repressed ideas attached to certain drives would bring us if they were to be allowed to become conscious (Laplanche and Pontalis 1973: 393–4).

2. Beyond Narrative

INTRODUCTION

So far, I have emphasised the tension between the diverse and contrary responses that an encounter with an artwork can elicit, and our experience of this diversity as still in some sense the responses of a particular self, encompassing as it does the connections and tensions between them. In the last chapter, I focused on Nietzsche's and Freud's accounts of this multiplicity in terms of the activity of drive processes. Nietzsche and Freud both understand these drives as simultaneously shaped in particular histories, at an individual and cultural level, and as shaping individuals and cultures, while Foucault extends this analysis to include the effects of power relations and the operation of various technologies.

The problem is what, if anything, allows us to interpret a manifold of feelings, reactions and activity as *ours*, and various interactive processes as contributing to the formation of a particular self? The problem of the unification of a self ranges both across the complexity of any given encounter and across time, in which processes of self-construction operate. Understandings of encounters with artworks in terms of a particular history, as for instance when we take ourselves to be moved by an image because it resonates with a memory of childhood, require us to connect experiences across time and ourselves to that child. While various activities and practices that we undertake project into the future and rely on the belief that we in some sense continue through time, even where we undertake practices explicitly aimed at changing ourselves. We have projects of the self that are orientated towards an idea of a future, if evolving, self.

So once we recognise the diversity of dynamic processes at work in shaping experiences, thoughts and actions, how do we avoid, as Ricoeur accuses both Hume and Nietzsche of doing, dismissing the subject as a mere illusion 'whose elimination merely brings to light a pure manifold of cognitions, emotions, and volitions' (Ricoeur 1988: 246). If we want to retain the idea of a self that unites this diversity, develops across time and has a future, then one approach to take is that a unification of this manifold occurs through storytelling, suggesting a narrative understanding of the self. It is to the possibilities and limits of narrative as a principle of self-unification that I turn in this chapter.

A strong narrative theory of the self claims more than that we have, as Peter Goldie puts it, a 'narrative sense of the self' that we employ and draw on in various activities and relationships (2012: 117). Rather, a 'strong narrativist' would maintain that the self is constituted by narratives and also generates these narratives (Teichert 2004: 183). This does not reduce the self to what is actually narrated; rather, as Marya Schechtman claims, herself an advocate of a narrative understanding of self-construction: 'no narrative view requires that we compose explicit and complete autobiographies in speech, writing, or thought' (Schechtman 2011: 407). The claim is rather that the telling of multiple stories, which may be in tension and may be both conscious and unconscious, weaves together a diversity of experiences, and makes sense of actions and choices. Our self-stories interweave with the stories of other people and employ the resources of cultural narratives. Through this process we form ourselves as a character, and interpret feelings, justify choices and incorporate changes in relation to this character, who we understand as persisting and developing over the course of a life story (even if this life story is never told from beginning to end). Narrative, it is claimed, thus draws together and unifies complex and diverse experiences, and lends us the continuity across time on which the significance of memory and hopes and plans for the future depend.

In order to fully assess a narrative approach to self-construction, I will first explore in detail Ricoeur's narrative theory of the self, before turning to consider what a narrative model might exclude and what distortions it might introduce in our understanding of self-construction. I will ultimately argue that, while a narrative sense of self in Goldie's sense is important to our self-understanding, and Ricoeur's theory of the self as constructed through emplotment has the advantage of accommodating complexity and change, the textual analogy in a narrative hermeneutics of the self does not adequately capture the multiplicity of interpretative processes of self-construction, or its bodily character. Nor does it allow for the possibility of a variety of forms which the unification of self-construction can take.

RICOEUR'S NARRATIVE THEORY OF THE SELF

I have chosen to examine Ricoeur as a representative of narrative approaches to self-construction because he offers a sophisticated analysis that recognises the complexity of self-construction and the constructed self. As Henry Venema notes, Ricoeur wants to account for a unifying process of ongoing self-construction, while still recognising the diversity that this activity incorporates (2000: 96). Plot, for Ricoeur, allows 'a synthesis of the heterogeneous' (1984: 66). Further, it is central to Ricoeur's account that establishing a narrative identity is a process. He emphasises that it depends on activity, and crucially this activity is never complete. Ricoeur aims at 'a model' which, as David Wood puts it, 'can accommodate the contingency and revisability of identity' (1991: 4). Ricoeur claims: 'narrative identity, constitutive of self-constancy, can include change, mutability, within the cohesion of one lifetime' (1988: 246). His approach to understanding self-construction thus contains crucial elements that I believe any successful account must accommodate, namely the presence of multiplicity involved in self-construction, the contingency of any unification between these diverse elements, the processual character of this unification, and thus the openness of a self undergoing construction to change.

Ricoeur's initial explorations of narrative are in the context of his exploration of the *aporia* that arises from the difference between our idea of cosmological or objective time, as a series of events, and our experience of phenomenological time, in which we have a sense of past, present and future. In his three-volume *Time and Narrative*, Ricoeur suggests narrative as a bridge between these two concepts of time, and narrative identity as the means of bridging historical and fictional narrative. It is in this context that he first posits narrative identity as a way of recognising a self that continues through time. Ricoeur argues that the 'mimetic activity of narrative' gives an individual or community a 'narrative identity' allowing an answer to the question 'who did this?' and 'justifies our taking the subject of an action, so designated by his, her, or its proper name, as the same throughout a life' (1988: 246). Ricoeur develops this idea of a narrative identity as a response to the inadequacy of analytic understandings of personal identity in an essay from 1991, where he argues that identity as a self [*ipse*] is not reducible to identity as sameness [*idem*] (1991b: 189). It is narrative identity that allows us to understand a self than can undergo change as persisting through time, without reducing this self to a 'what' or substance. This notion of narrative identity is articulated in greater detail, in relation to the problem of agency and our relationship to others, in *Oneself as Another*, published in 1992. Here, Ricoeur is concerned with the importance of narrative for understanding ourselves as ethical agents.

How then does Ricoeur think narrative allows us to answer the question of 'who did that'? and to understand ourselves as selves, with a past, present and future? We must begin with Ricoeur's understanding of narrative in terms of the activity of emplotment, which he draws from Aristotle's poetics. 'Emplotment' is 'the synthesis of heterogeneous elements' (Ricoeur 1991a: 21), in which the poet achieves 'the triumph of concordance over discordance' (Ricoeur 1984: 31). These elements are the disparate events that are connected by the narrative arc into a meaningful whole. The organisation of events into a plot 'allows us to integrate with permanence in time what seems to be its contrary in the domain of sameness-identity, namely diversity, variability, discontinuity and instability' (Ricoeur 1992: 140). It occurs in three overlapping and mutually reinforcing stages – prefiguration, configuration and refiguration – which I will discuss in turn.

Prefiguration refers to the fact that Emplotment, or narrative composition, is anchored 'in the symbolic resources of the practical field' (Ricoeur 1984: 57). Thus, narrative is not something the *mimetic* activity of the writer arbitrarily imposes on human life. Novels and plays are only possible because of a 'prenarrative quality' (Ricoeur 1992: 157), that is present 'in the fundamental structures of practical experience' (Venema 2000: 98). These structures include our experience of time: 'we recognize temporal structures which call for narrative' (Ricoeur 1984: 59). Ricoeur writes in the first volume of *Time and Narrative*: 'If, in fact, human action can be narrated, it is because it is always already articulated by signs, rules, norms' (1984: 57). The world of human practices and actions is not a chaos of happenings but is already structured by us and subject to various rules of action and interpretation. 'Symbolism confers an initial readability on action [. . .] If we may nevertheless speak of action as a quasi-text, it is insofar as the symbols, understood as interpretants, provide the rules of meaning as a function of which this or that behavior can be interpreted' (Ricoeur 1984: 58).

Given this prenarrative character of life, an imaginative configuration is possible, in which a writer can bestow unity on diversity, creating 'discordant concordance' in a creative act (Ricoeur 1984: 42). The novelist or dramatist displays a 'power of unification unfurled by the configuring act constituting *poiēsis* itself' (Ricoeur 1992: 142). In this poetic unification, contingent events are bestowed with narrative necessity in the context of an overarching plot:

> The paradox of emplotment is that it inverts the effect of contingency, in the sense of that which could have happened differently or which might not have happened at all, by incorporating it in some way into the effect of necessity or probability exerted by the configuring act [. . .] This necessity is a narrative necessity whose meaning effect comes from the configuring act as such. (Ricoeur 1992: 142)

In Ricoeur's analysis of Aristotle's art of composition the events of a plot are connected logically in terms of 'an intelligibility appropriate to the field of *praxis*' (Ricoeur 1984: 40). While prefiguration enables or determines the terms of meaning of this configuration, Ricoeur is clear that it is only in the poetic act of organisation into a whole – with a beginning, middle and end that are 'not features of some real action but the effects of the ordering of the poem' – that the events are internally connected by narrative necessity (Ricoeur 1984: 39). '[T]he possible and the general are not to be sought elsewhere than in the organization of the events, since it is this linkage that has to be necessary or probable' (Ricoeur 1984: 41).

Emplotment, however, the 'structuration' of heterogenous elements into a discordant concordance, 'is only completed in the spectator or the reader' (Ricoeur 1984: 48). It requires an imaginative act of synthesis. Or as Ricoeur puts it in 'Life in Quest of Narrative', the 'integrating process' of the plot is 'is completed only in the reader or in the spectator, that is to say in the *living* receiver of the narrated story' (1991a: 21). For Aristotle, with whom Ricoeur's analysis of emplotment begins, the completeness of the work is attested to by its effect on the reader, or the pleasure it induces in them, and Ricoeur argues, 'this pleasure is both constructed in the work and made actual outside it. It joins inside to outside and requires us to treat in a dialectical fashion this relation of outside to inside' (1984: 48). The pleasure taken in 'recognition' and in 'the composition as necessary or probable', is 'both constructed in the piece and exercised by the spectator' (Ricoeur 1984: 49). What is probable depends on what we as readers find persuasive or convincing in the text. 'Hence, by its very nature, the intelligibility characteristic of dissonant concordance – what Aristotle puts under the term "probable" – is the common product of the work and the public. The persuasive is born at their intersection' (Ricoeur 1984: 50). And of course the emotions of fear and pity essential to Aristotle's understanding of tragedy must be experienced by the spectator, though this experience depends on the play's construction. Thus 'the dialectic of inside and outside reaches its highest point in catharsis' (Ricoeur 1984: 50).

Crucially, Ricoeur makes the further claim that this dialectic depends on the work deploying 'a world that the reader appropriates. This world is a cultural world' (1991a: 26). We, therefore, in refiguration return full circle to the way in which literature informs the meaning of the field of action in a way that makes the representation of action, completed in our reading of it, possible. Ricoeur embraces this circle in which literature can inform and transform life:

> the process of composition, of configuration, is not completed in the text but in the reader and, under this condition, makes possible the reconfiguration of life by narrative. I should say, more precisely: the sense or the significance of a narrative stems from the *intersection of the world of the text and the world of the reader*. The act of reading then becomes the critical moment of the entire analysis. On it rests the narrative's capacity to transfigure the experience of the reader. (Ricoeur 1991a: 26)

The capacity to affect the world of the reader is crucial for the transposition of emplotment in literature to the emplotment of life in narrative identity.

How though does plot relate to the question of the self? We have already seen that Ricoeur argues that narrative identity can succeed in accounting for personal identity across time in a way that does not reduce identity to sameness but is rather the identity of a self. The narrative self has a constancy across time that can accommodate change in the same way that a character can undertake, and be subject to, various actions in the course of a story and can be understood to develop in the course of this story. The notion of character development depends on the assumption that it is the same character who now behaves in a way, or holds beliefs, that they would not have done at the start of the novel or play. 'Understood in narrative terms, identity can be called by linguistic convention, the identity of the *character*' (Ricoeur 1992: 141). 'By "character"', Ricoeur writes, 'I understand the set of distinctive marks which permit the reidentification of a human individual as being the same' (1992: 119). Character 'designates the set of lasting dispositions by which a person is recognized' (Ricoeur 1992: 121). In the notion of character, literature thus furnishes us with an answer to the question of how a self that is not reducible to sameness can yet be the *same* person that they were many years ago, and before many life-changing experiences. Narrative 'produces a dialectic of the character which is quite clearly a dialectic of sameness and selfhood' (Ricoeur 1992: 140–1).

Plot relates to personal identity because character is the means by which we can establish a self that can be identified and re-identified yet is not reduced to the sameness of a thing, and character is constructed in the act of emplotment: 'The narrative constructs the identity of the character [. . .] it is the identity of the story which makes the identity of the character' (Ricoeur 1992: 147–8). Ricoeur describes this process in terms of a dialectic in which:

> the character draws his or her singularity from the unity of a life considered a temporal totality which is itself singular and distinguished from all others. Following the line of discordance, this temporal totality is threatened by the disruptive effect of the unforeseeable events that punctuate it (encounters, accidents, etc.). Because of the concordant discordant synthesis this contingency of the event contributes to the necessity, retroactive so to speak, of the history of a life, to which is equated the identity of the character. Thus chance is transmuted into fate. (1992: 147)

We understand the character in a story in terms of the totality of events that befall them and the actions that they take. But we can understand this story as a totality only with the help of characters.

Hence, Ricoeur suggests that just as character depends on plot, plot in turn depends on character:

> it is the characters who preside over the unity of the subset of functions that allows action to become more complicated and the quest to develop further. We might ask in this respect whether all emplotment does not really arise out of the mutual genesis of a character's development and the development of a story. (1985: 37)

Ultimately, Ricoeur expresses this mutual dependence in terms of an interconnected identity: 'the character preserves throughout the story an identity correlative to that of the story itself' (1992: 143). The identity of the story, as a concordant discordance, is always at stake in the narrative arc. There is a 'competition between a demand for concordance and the admission of discordances which, up to the close of the story, threaten this identity' (Ricoeur 1992: 141). Character is part of what holds this tenuous and vulnerable unity together by providing a framework in which we understand the events gathered together in the narrative as necessary or probable. We understand actions as in character or out of character, and events as affecting and shaping a character, and this rescues them from being an arbitrary succession of episodes, instead giving them meaningful connections. This is demonstrated by the limit cases. In novels that explore the loss of identity there is also a loss of narrative structure. In discussing Robert Musil's *The Man Without Qualities*, Ricoeur suggests: 'as the novel approaches this annulling of the person in terms of sameness-identity, the novel also loses its properly narrative qualities' (1991b: 196).

The relevance of narrative to the problem of how we can recognise a self as the same while still incorporating heterogeneous elements is thus clear in the notion of character and the interdependence of character with plot. The question is now how the model as explored in literature can be applied to life. What is involved in the creation of myself as a character with my life history? As with the account of literature, this will be a creative, dynamic process but it will occur throughout my life. In his commentary on Ricoeur, Venema stresses that '[t]he selection of significant meanings that are to become representative of who I am involves a highly complex procedure spread out over the course of my life' (2000: 97). Crucially, this involves the three stages of emplotment I discussed in relation to literature operating in a reinforcing circle. This is a circle that Ricoeur is fully aware of but maintains to be inevitable and not vicious. We have already seen that for Ricoeur life prefigures narrative, but that in turn literature feeds back into life, reinforcing 'a process of symbolization already at work' (Carr, Taylor, Ricoeur 1992: 182). Thus, the construction of the self uses cultural symbols, including those that we take from traditions of storytelling and literature (Ricoeur 1991a: 35). 'What is prefigured in our life results from refigurations operated by all the other lives of those who taught us' (Carr et al. 1991: 182). Reading provides models for actions and identity. Hence, it transforms us, and we in turn transform the field of action in which others form their identity and act in a way that, already organised and laden with meaning, these actions can be represented in literature. It is because, as Venema clearly sums it up, '[w]ith Reading, narrative meaning is appropriated from the virtual world of the text and incorporated into the actual world of the reader' (2000: 102), that the construction of narrative identity is possible. And thus, '[n]arrative configuration is completed through an act of reading that produces a possibility for experience which, when taken up through decision and action, refigures experiences and therein personal identity' (Venema 2000: 103).

The problem of how literature and life connect is not therefore unique to narrative identity, because for Ricoeur the intersection of the world of the text and the world of the reader is already an integral part of the possibility of creating and comprehending narrative in literature, and literature is already part of a hermeneutic circle in which it feeds back into the structures of our lives, including our sense of self. However, it is important to note, as Ricoeur himself does, that there are important differences between the creation for each of us of our own narrative identity and the creation of a character in a novel. Ricoeur suggests that these differences can be incorporated into a proper understanding of narrative identity rather than implying a breakdown of the analogy between the self and a literary character.

Ricoeur acknowledges that when we create our narrative identity through the active narration of our lives there is no clear beginning or end as there is in a piece of literature. Thus, there is no total and final narrative in terms of which the unity of plot – and in relation to this unity the identity of our character – is understood. Rather there is an 'open-ended incomplete, imperfect mediation' (Ricoeur 1988: 207). This revisability in which identity is established through the mutual dependence of a narrated plot and its character – but is always continually re-established – is something that Ricoeur takes as a positive of his narrative understanding of identity, which can account for the mutability of the self. But while there is no fixed totality with the beginning and end that a novel possesses, one that as Ricoeur points out is not necessarily the same as a linear historical succession but rather a beginning according to the poetic intention of the author, a looser notion of beginnings and endings is helpful to us in our lived experience. The literary sense of beginning and end offers us a tool that helps us in life:

> with the help of narrative beginnings which our reading has made familiar to us, straining this somewhat, we stabilize the real beginning formed by the initiatives (in the strong sense of the term) that we take. And we also have the experience, however incomplete, of what is meant by ending a course of action, a slice of life. Literature helps us in a sense to fix the outline of these provisional ends. (Ricoeur 1992: 162)

Ricoeur is also very clear that we are not the authors of our lives, stating: 'We can become our own narrator, in imitation of these narrative voices, without being able to become the author. This is the great difference between life and fiction' (1991a: 32). And later: we can be '[n]arrator and character, perhaps, but of a life of which, unlike the creatures of fiction, I am not the author but at most, to use Aristotle's expression, the co-author, the *sunaition*' (1992: 160). We neither bring ourselves into existence nor determine, as Jean-Paul Sartre would call it, our particular 'facticity', the place, time, of our birth, etc., rather than the meaning we give to them (2003: 103–8). We are also not in control of many of the things that happen to us. Ricoeur rejects the idea that he attributes to Alasdair MacIntyre (2007 [1985]) that life histories are *enacted* narratives. Ricoeur goes on to say: 'But should not the equivocalness of the author's position be preserved rather than dissipated? By narrating a life of which I am not the author as to existence, I make myself its co-author as to its meaning' (1992: 162). We don't make our narratives through our actions as much as in our interpretations (though of course interpretation is an activity). We give meaning to our actions, and to the events and actions of others that affect us, through our self-understanding in terms of the narrative of our life. The act of emplotment is the act of interpretation of our life history as a history that can be narrated, in which we operate as a character in that story.

It is not quite as simple, however, as saying that the author of a novel invents with total freedom whereas the narrator of a life must restrict themselves to the interpretation of the material that is given to them. The difference in Ricoeur's account is more one of degree. For an author of a novel to be able to engage in mimetic activity, they must represent the intelligible field of human life that is already culturally structured. While the narrator of a life, who is also the character of that life, does contribute to that narrative through choices and actions they take, as well as in their selection and description of significant events and actions. They also, as a member of their culture, collectively contribute to the developing field of signification in which they deliberate and act, through refiguration. This refiguration occurs both in their uptake of cultural stories, their engagement with literature and its narratives, and in their reading of their own life. Thus, '[t]he Subject then appears both as a reader and the writer of its own life, as Proust would have it' (Ricoeur 1988: 246).

Finally, something we have already touched on in considering that we are not the God-like authors of our lives, or by implication of our narrated identity as the character of those lives, is the recognition that we are always entangled with others, affecting them and affected by them. The self is always constructed in a cultural context. As Schechtman notes there are:

> constraints on our self-narratives. We are not composing the stories of our lives in a vacuum, but in a world where there are others with their own stories about themselves and about us [. . .] Both because our narratives must make reference to the stories available to us from the traditions in which we find ourselves and because they must interact with the realities of the world in which we live and the narratives of others, our narratives must be understood as embedded in a world of other selves. (2011: 405)

We have seen that for Ricoeur this dependence on others was already true to a certain extent in the production and reading of literature. Writers must also make reference to the stories available in their traditions. So, this does not, for Ricoeur, suggest a sharp rupture between life and literature. In his account of Aristotle's poetics, the circular process, in which literature shapes the field of action the poet represents and the act of emplotment is completed in the refiguration effected by the reader who impacts back on that field of action, the role of a shared cultural context is apparent. So, whether in literature or in life, interpretation and reinterpretation are always 'in the light of the narratives proposed to us by our culture' (1991a: 32). Given the dependence of emplotment on the intersection of the world of the novel and the world of the reader, the writer of the novel does not have total autonomy from others. But in writing their novel and having the characters behave in certain ways, the author does not have to take account of actual others in the same way that Ricoeur understands we must, i.e. as ethical agents who consider others in our actions. We must, as Schechtman says, react to the realities and narratives of others that we encounter. Hence, our self-narrative will always be in the context not just of our actions but also *inter*actions.

In Ricoeur's theory, therefore, we have a subtle account of self-construction, which recognises that this occurs in a cultural context and in interaction with others, and it aims to incorporate heterogeneous elements in a way that can accommodate ongoing change. Importantly, this theory does not simply impose a literary analogy onto life but suggests a continuously self-reinforcing hermeneutic circle in which our reading of literature informs our possible actions, which inform our narrative possibilities, which in turn inform our cultural body of literature. Ricoeur presents a powerful account for how narrative operates as a part of human life. Narrative identity does seem to offer an interpretative unity, with which we can understand ourselves as agents with life projects, that succeeds in incorporating diversity and is open to revision. But if we take narrative as a 'privileged mediation' in self-interpretation, as Ricoeur suggests, what do we neglect and what possibilities do we foreclose (1991b: 188)?

THE LIMITS OF NARRATIVE

We have now examined in detail how Ricoeur's account of the self in terms of a narrative identity, constructed through the emplotment of our life history, suggests that we can establish a continuous agency through the interpretation of ourselves as a character within this plot. So, on Ricoeur's narrative approach, the self is constructed through the process of narrative interpretation, from activity and experiences that can be incorporated into a plot and ultimately expressed in language. The material of self-construction, to use an expression Ricoeur himself applies to human action (Ricoeur 1984: 58), is hence treated as 'quasi-text' – it is always open to being read.

But is an understanding of the hermeneutics of the self entirely in terms of the narrative interpretation of a 'quasi-text' adequate? This 'quasi-text' is not, for Ricoeur, something that is simply given, or there prior to human cultural and artistic activity. As Venema stresses, the self for Ricoeur is a task (2000: 158). So Ricoeur is not suggesting an underlying text of the self that hermeneutic activity simply reveals. He is not guilty of positing a 'true' self that hermeneutic interpretation provides the key to deciphering. There is no self that is prior to the activity of interpretation, construed in terms of the unifying act of telling a story that establishes a character in mutual dependency with plot. Nor is the process of emplotment and thus the creation of narrative identity ever complete; it is an ongoing and revisable process. And, crucially, we have seen how this process involves others and is embedded in a cultural context. Without the figuration of the cultural field in symbolic, prenarrative terms, the actions and events of our life history could not be plotted such that we produce ourselves as characters. Thus, Ricoeur's sophisticated theory of the narrative self avoids some of the potential pitfalls of an analogy with the novel. Ricoeur does not make us the God-like author of ourselves with total power over the narrative that we weave. Nor does he reduce the self to a text already composed and standing in need of revelation, and thus inevitably always out of reach. Hence, he does not employ the supposition of a hidden self, which Foucault argues has been exploited in power strategies (Foucault 1978).

For Ricoeur, however, these processes of emplotment, although incomplete and cooperative, are always understood according to the analogy of writing and reading a literary text. For Ricoeur 'selfhood is situated in the semantic world of the text' (Venema 2000: 158). Ricoeur is careful to acknowledge our fundamental embodiment, but does the literary analogy inevitably neglect or distort how corporeality is involved in our self-construction?

Narrative theories of the self have been accused of neglecting the importance of embodiment with subsequent attempts made at correcting this. Catriona Mackenzie, while acknowledging that both Ricoeur and Schechtman insist on the embodiment of the narrative self, and that Ricoeur pays attention to this, sets out to better characterise this embodiment (2009: 2014). Mackenzie accepts the idea of narrative self-construction but argues that 'subjectivity is actively constituted against the background of and in relation to the life of the body' (2009: 117), and that we therefore need an adequate explanation of embodiment as part of an account of the process of self-construction through narration (2009, 2014). Mackenzie suggests that 'our self-narratives must incorporate an ongoing yet changing bodily perspective [. . .] The bodily perspective, as I understand it, encompasses both the lived experience of one's body as a whole, and of parts of one's body, and the subjective meaning or significance sef that experience in the context of one's narrative self-conception' (2014: 162). She suggests further that our lived bodily experience is always already mediated via narrative self-interpretation (Mackenzie 2014: 162). Pricilla Brandon extends this work in exploring how the body and narrative interact, and how 'narrative self-image' can influence and shape the body (2016: 74).

As Diana Tietjens Meyers argues, however, there are aspects of bodily experience that defy incorporation into narrative and semantic articulation. There is, Meyers insists, 'nonconceptual content that the lived body is imbued with and that it also generates and expresses' (Meyers 2013: 147). Thus, there are various activities, sensations and processes that seem to escape linguistic capture. We may try to describe our embodied sensations and movements, but words are not adequate to the task. We all know what it is like to have a sensation that we cannot describe, or to sense processes and forces that elude our attempts to articulate or represent them. We may use words to gesture towards or indicate the presence of such phenomena, but something is always lost in translation.

Mackenzie responds to Meyers's concern that narrative excludes non-conceptual bodily meaning, agreeing with her, and with Merleau-Ponty,[1] that 'there are forms of self-awareness, self-experience, self-knowledge, self-understanding and self-expression that are primarily bodily and non-inferential, rather than linguistic and conceptual' (Mackenzie 2014: 163).[2] Mackenzie gives the example of the experience, and bodily expression, of affects such as grief and anger. But while Mackenzie accepts that meaning and understanding can be encoded in the body, she argues that narrative agency and bodily experience are interwoven (Mackenzie 2014: 164). The process of narrative self-constitution which she puts forward as an account of self-construction is not, according to Mackenzie, the narration of a prenarrative bodily experience. I am sympathetic to the idea expressed here, that to allege that narrative self-construction fails to successfully articulate or translate bodily experience seems to problematically separate the continual constitution of the body and its experiences and the continual constitution of the self. The problem is not in my view that language fails to fully capture or articulate non-conceptual, or non-semantic, somatic experience conceived of as inert, pre-existing material to be incorporated more or less successfully into a constructed self. But I agree with Meyers that Mackenzie's account 'over-estimates the reach of narrative' (Meyers 2013: 142). What is it then that narrative cannot reach? It is worth noting that Meyers does not just mention the non-conceptual content the body is 'imbued with' but also that which it *generates*. The point is there are non-semantic *processes* of interpretation which should not be excluded from our understanding of the *process(es)* of self-construction. These include for instance muscle memory, which need only contingently become conscious but which contributes to forming a self. Mackenzie is right to recognise that body and self are interwoven, and influence each other, but the idea of body she employs is already by her own admission one that fits the narrative mould. Referring to 'bodily gestures, habits, bearing and personal style' she argues 'that what the person thereby expresses bodily is herself, as body-subject and concretely individuated, temporally extended narrative agent' (Mackenzie 2014: 163). This treats the body as something clearly individuated, and already determined by narrative agency, even in its non-conceptual and non-semantic expressions, rather than recognising a plurality of somatic interpretations as part of self-construction.

As I argued in Chapter 1, however, a wide variety of practices and processes contribute to a hermeneutics of the self. We saw in Chapter 1 that one way this multiple activity can be understood is as the activity of corporeal drives. Nietzsche argues for an understanding of the complexity and variability of our experience in terms of which drive, in a shifting alliance of drives, is currently dominant, or how a particular symbiotic relationship operates. Thus, he proposes it is our drives which interpret the world, claiming '[i]t is our needs *which interpret the world*; our drives and their for and against' (Nietzsche 1988: vol. 12, 315), and '[o]ur waking life is an interpretation of inner drive processes' (Nietzsche 1988: vol. 9, 216). The Nietzschean explanation of the complexity of our experience in terms of a plurality of interpretative activity is distinct from Ricoeur's insight that a text, and human action taken as a 'quasi-text', has many possible interpretations or readings. Rather, a hermeneutics of the self on Nietzsche's understanding of hermeneutics involves the actual interaction of different extant interpretative processes. We need to explain how the simultaneous presence of multiple interpretations can be unified. On this view, tracing how a self comes into existence involves exploring the interactive activity of the drives and the history which shapes them, as well as the social and cultural practices they give rise to in interaction with others, and the power structures these interactions establish. The problem, therefore, is that if narrative is presented as the sole means by which the diversity of our experience is interpreted to form a self, this misconstrues the somatic and plural nature of interpretation, and hence misconstrues the hermeneutics of the self and the self that emerges from it.

If we move beyond literature as a model of self-construction, then we can bring our attention to interpretative processes that do not take linguistic or story form and that cannot be woven together into such a form. A hermeneutics of the self can then more fully acknowledge and employ our bodily processes. With Ricoeur we already leave behind the Cartesian reduction of self to pure, isolated thought and recognise the self as something that is made in an interactive and culturally structured process. A narrative theory of self-construction, however, cannot account for the plurality of interpretative bodily activity.

Thus, despite admitting the role of interpretation, we remain trapped in the same denial and suppression of body, and multiple and continuous bodily interpretations, that Nietzsche analyses as running from Plato's criticisms of the 'lovers of sights and sounds' in *The Republic* (Plato 1997: 1102), through Christianity, and into the valorisation of objectivity in the '*ideal* scholar'. Nietzsche accuses such an objective type of becoming only a mirror unable to know themselves and 'wrong about his own basic needs' (2002: 97–8). If our self-interpretation cannot incorporate the interpretative activity of corporeal drives it will remain, as Nietzsche claims of his contemporary culture, at the level of something 'stuck on like a paper flower or poured over like icing-sugar' (1997: 117), unable to express or unite the heterogenous processes it obscures. It is not enough to recognise the presence of interpretation – the somatic and plural character of interpretation must also be recognised. A broader understanding of hermeneutics is thus required which escapes the literary analogy and which recognises the diversity and corporeality of interpretative processes. Otherwise we escape the trap of 'objective truth' for another distorting and limiting trap in the form of narrative.

In addition to taking an overly narrow view of the processes of self-construction, the model of emplotment takes a narrow view regarding the possible forms of selfhood, or what could constitute a unity of style between diverse elements. Here Meyers suggests, while rejecting the overall framework of his approach, that Galen Strawson hits upon a useful notion in the concept of 'form-finding' (Meyers 2013: 150). In his critique of narrative theories of selfhood Strawson argues that storytelling is just one species of possible 'form-finding' (2004: 442). I would suggest that we might better term the processes of possible self-unification as 'form-giving' or 'form-creating' but agree that plot is just one possible way in which such form or unification could be created. Or, to use Nietzsche's language of giving style to one's character (2001: 163), literary style need not be the only way we can understand stylistic unity. Plot need not be the only form through which a synthesis of heterogeneous elements, and processes, can be achieved. Thus, the self need not be equated with character. We can turn to other art practices to see how a unity of artistic style can take many, and non-linear, forms, employing for instance shape, colour, texture, movement, mood and feeling.

So narrative offers us a powerful way to understand how the self can be formed in a continual process, such that it can be identified across time, but it also threatens to ignore the diversity of interpretative processes that can contribute to our self-formation, and limit our self-expression and who we can become. We have both the worry that emplotment, or the activity of interpreting our life *story* as a meaningful and *readable* whole, cannot incorporate the multitude of active and bodily sensations or interpretations that contribute to our becoming who we are, and the concern that 'plot' is too limiting an account of the form that 'who we are' can take.

BEYOND LITERATURE

Given the limitations of the narrative paradigm drawn from literature, what alternatives do non-literary art practices open up? Crucially practices such as sculpture, performance and painting can underscore the significance of the corporeal, at the same time as interrogating the role the body plays in relation to identity. We can see this if we compare how the vulnerability or even annulment of self is experienced in literature and in visual art. Ricoeur rightly identifies that literature can explore the disintegration of self, as well as providing a model for its unification (1991b: 196). How does this compare to the way in which Ernst van Alphen suggests that Francis Bacon's paintings induce a loss of self in the viewer (van Alphen 1993: 10)?

Bacon's work is raw, infused with the violence that surrounded him both politically, spanning two world wars and the Troubles in Ireland, and personally. While his contemporaries moved increasingly towards abstractions, Bacon's work focuses almost entirely on the human form or figure. He turned to the figurative works of past masters like Velázquez, Rembrandt, Van Gogh and Picasso, made use of Muybridge's photography of athletes, and produced multiple portraits of friends, lovers and himself.

Yet while Bacon eschews abstraction, he also saw himself as striving to get beyond a merely illustrative approach, in search of an image with 'a greater reality' (Sylvester 1980: 107). In dialogue with Bacon, David Sylvester teases out what Bacon is seeking as 'trying to make an image of appearance that is conditioned as little as possible by the accepted standards of what appearance is' (Sylvester 1980: 105). Bacon seeks to go beyond, or penetrate, the frameworks of illustration, representation, narrative and identity. Yet he cannot escape them entirely. Reflecting on his own art practice Bacon says that perhaps he is trying to achieve the 'impossible':

in spite of theoretically longing for the image to be made up of irrational marks, inevitably illustration has to come into it to make certain parts of the head and face which, if one left them out, one would then only be making an abstract design. (Slyvester 1980: 126)

Bacon thus simultaneously suggests and undermines conventions of meaning as semantic or representational. He employs and subverts the nude's history in figurative art in which we expect a clearly defined figure to be painted on the canvas. Instead of meeting our expectations, the somatic presence of flesh and indeterminacy of any discrete bodily figure disrupts the paradigm of figurative art and representational meaning.

In the case of narrative, van Alphen argues that by employing multiple figures (which suggest the possibility of interaction), the three-part form of triptychs (indicating the possibility of temporal continuity between panels), and the visible brush strokes of his figures (suggesting movement), Bacon pulls us towards a narrative reading of his work (van Alphen 1993: 23–4). Yet at the same time, narrative is something Bacon rejects in interpretations of his work and seeks to undermine in the work itself (Sylvester 1980: 63–5). His figures are isolated in distinct and contemporaneous spaces, defeating their configuration as characters in a continuous and coherent story (van Alphen 1993: 29). Several of his best-known works, for example *Three Studies for a Crucifixion* (1962), are triptychs consisting of three separate canvases. While van Alphen suggests this allows a reading of temporal continuity between the panels, Bacon, responding to Sylvester's question concerning the function of the vertical breaks between the different canvases in a triptych, answers '[t]hey isolate from the other. And they cut off the story between one and the other. It helps to avoid story-telling if the figures are painted on three different canvases' (Sylvester 1980: 23). His use of the triptych to create distinct sections thus aims to 'negate any narrative' (Deleuze 2017: xiv).

At the same time as this disruption of narrative, Bacon questions the boundaries of the self in his work. He paints figures, including many recognisable portraits. But Bacon's figures are often disfigured: distorted, dismembered and dissolving. They bleed into and merge with their surroundings. Van Alphen suggests too that the viewer's sense of self is disrupted when engaging with Bacon's work, through the very violence and power of the images. In his commentary on Bacon, van Alphen is in fact setting out to explain why it hurts to look at Bacon's work, claiming that we are 'drawn and drowned inside' his paintings (van Alphen 1993: 10).

Thus, narrative is both evoked and explicitly undermined in Bacon's work and at the same time selfhood is expressed and experienced as tenuous and on the verge of dissipation. Thus, the lack of self is still equated to a lack of plot in the way in which Ricoeur suggests narrative and identity break down together in modernist literature. In the connection between narrative disintegration and loss of self, narrative and identity remain connected. What then does the figurative painting add to our experience of the loss of self that is not offered by for example Musil?

Bacon's paintings have a visceral effect on the viewer's senses; he aims to address our nervous system directly (Deleuze 2017: 37; Sylvester 1980: 18, 58–9). The way in which Bacon's works assault our senses and threaten our sense of self in their violence is a sensual and bodily process. The vulnerability of the self is then felt not just as a conceptual problem of fragmented identity but in terms of the vulnerability and porosity of bodies. Bacon's figures are open to penetration and emission. In discussing a Degas pastel Bacon suggests the force of the image is in the top of the spine almost breaking through the skin (Sylvester 1980: 46–7). In his own *Three Figures and Portrait* (1975, Figure 2.1), the figure on the left contorts backwards, the flesh falling back to expose the arc of the spinal column. His figures convey this sense of the body breaking through and spilling out. In *Three Studies for a Crucifixion* (1962), bodies bleed and skeletal structures are exposed. Bacon's are figures which can be impaled and injured, made to bleed, and more profanely they also vomit and defecate (for instance, in *Triptych*, May–June 1973 and *Three Figures in a Room*, 1964). But we do not just suffer the bodily effects of being confronted by Bacon's visceral and disturbing works, we also identify with the bodies. We feel ourselves as vulnerable flesh. Bacon's paintings not only carry a threat of a loss of self in the form of psychological disintegration, which they share with literature, but also in bodily dismemberment. Loss of self as a Dionysiac rending is evoked. In an interview with Sylvester, and in the paintings themselves, Bacon reminds us that 'we are meat, we are potential carcasses' (Sylvester 1980: 46). In reminding us that we are flesh, in connecting the loss of self with the dismemberment or decomposition of flesh, Bacon reminds us of the importance of the corporeality of any self-construction.

Bacon does not suggest that the converse of this association between the disintegration of body with the disintegration of self is that the integrity of the body automatically bestows an integrity of identity. As van Alphen argues, 'Bacon's bodies hinder any attempt to derive from them a sense of an existence, identity or solidity' (1993: 114). The line between the body and the outside blurs in Bacon: 'the space

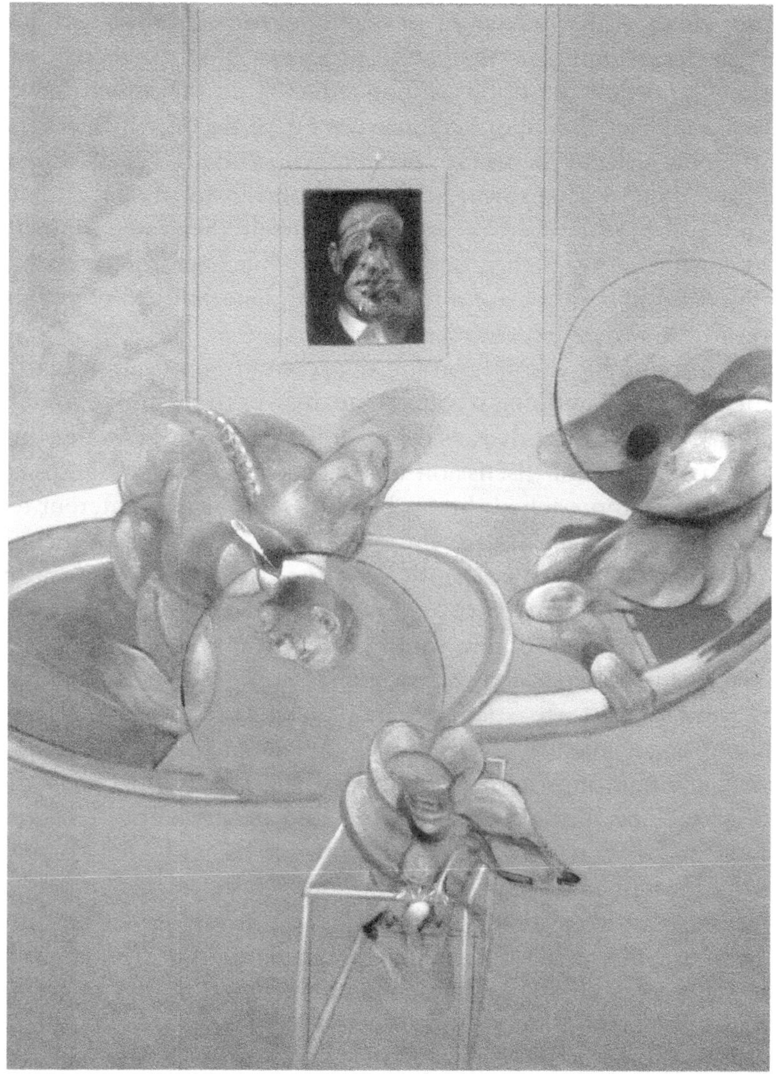

2.1 Francis Bacon, *Three Figures and Portrait*, 1975, oil paint and pastel on
canvas, 198.1 × 147.3 cm.
© The Estate of Francis Bacon. All rights reserved. DACS 2021

surrounding the body comes to hold bodily qualities, into which body
decomposes' (van Alphen 193: 162). Neither the body nor its representation in figurative art or in narrative literature solve the problem
of fragmented identity. We still need an account of the form-giving
or unifying processes that establish a self. Bacon's work concerns
an intimation of a bodily reality that enters at the point where the
frameworks of representation and identity break down. Bacon does

not provide us with an account of or model for self-construction, but his work does remind us that these processes must be recognised to be bodily, and that the bodily is not reducible to the figure. Sylvester makes a comment in one of his interviews with Bacon which resonates with the Nietzschean dictum to 'become who you are', suggesting that artists are often striving towards 'this idea of transforming the material very radically in order to make it more like itself' (Sylvester 1980: 126). (Self)-transformation is then never arbitrary but operates according to the limits and possibilities of a fundamental materiality, a theme that I will return to in the next chapter.

Ricoeur found the inspiration for an account of unification in drama and the novel, and in doing so offered an answer to the problem of how we can understand ourselves as agents with a past, present and future. But in starting with a discussion of an encounter with *The Disasters of War*, I have approached the problem of self-unity in different terms which suggest the need for a solution other than plot. Our encounter with Goya's etchings is not static, but the problem of unification it presents is not the problem of connecting actions at different points in time as the actions of the same person, but rather of connecting concurrent but diverse activity or interpretations as all contributing to the formation of a particular self. Crucially, this diverse activity is felt in our engagement with disturbing images such as Goya's etchings and Bacon's paintings as *bodily* activity and sensation. Our sensible reactions include physical disturbances and excitements. Artists such as Goya and Bacon articulate and confront us with our corporeality. A hermeneutics of the self which does justice to this corporeality cannot interpret it entirely within the model of text and story. It will be a hermeneutics of the self in which interpretation is diversified, both in the sense of allowing simultaneous interpretation and in terms of a broader understanding of interpretation than one which equates it with establishing the meaning of a text. Emplotment is only one strand in the complex processes in which we currently establish who we are, and one possible route towards selfhood. If emplotment is taken as the only process of forming a self, then we exclude the multiplicity of interpretations and their bodily nature, which we feel so keenly when we contemplate the work of Goya or Bacon. In order to be able to incorporate the excess which does not fit the template of a plot, and which Bacon evokes at the margins of figurative representation, we must move towards a hermeneutics of the self that recognises a plurality of interpretative processes and their corporeal nature.

CONCLUSION

There are elements of Ricoeur's analysis that it is worth taking forward. Firstly, the case for the importance that narrative plays in much of our self-understanding is clear. Narrative is a highly significant part of human culture, and we do tell ourselves stories that make sense of our experiences and justify our actions. In particular, narrative plays an important role in many practices of self-cultivation. This can operate on the level of understanding why we take up a particular practice, projecting into the future the idea of a self that is improved by this practice, or it can occur where narratives actually form an explicit part of the practice and its aims. This is the case when, for example, a talking therapy aims to change our self-narrative by encouraging us to take ownership of our actions or to see painful experiences as learning experiences; the goal is to get us to tell a different story. However, we can incorporate narrative as *an* important process in self-construction without reducing self-construction to the process of emplotment. Indeed, visual artworks which involve narrative elements but also exhibit visual features and material features dependent on the media of construction can help us understand how a process of self-construction can operate as a diverse material process and can incorporate both narrative and non-narrative forms of interpretation. Crucially, Ricoeur's particular account of narrative identity in relation to the dynamic process of emplotment has also shown the role that artworks can have in contributing to the field of possible actions and self-formation. Our interpretations of artworks feed back into our cultural world, providing models for identity and for action. Art is potentially transformative because it already intersects with the world of the audience. Finally, Ricoeur is right to emphasise that this process is one that involves an interaction between the artist and the audience.

I will address the transformative possibilities of art in the context of resisting being tied to particular identities, and thus challenging the ossification of the power structures they are complicit with, in Chapters 4 and 5. To limit ourselves to literature, and to narrative or symbolic readings of other art forms, however, is to limit the possibilities of artworks. If the processes of self-construction are recognised to range beyond the activity of emplotment, then the range of artworks that we see as having the potential to transfigure us is also widened. Audience receptions of sculpture, performance, installations, paintings and photography allow new understandings of body, appropriation of imagery, new experiences of seeing and being seen, explorations of boundaries between the body and the world it moves in, and experimentation in what constitutes unification of diverse processes to constitute a self. These new insights or models can disrupt power structures and open up new forms of selfhood.

In the next chapter, I aim to explore a hermeneutics of the self which escapes the narrative trap and does justice to the corporeality of processes of self-construction by turning to visual art, and the work of Louise Bourgeois in particular. Her works, ranging from non-specific biomorphic shapes to figurative pieces, give us insight into how form can be created from multiple, material processes, and incorporate diverse and even conflicting interpretations. The forms that emerge and their signification, depend on their materials, and we see that these materials have their own directional tendencies. The artist does not simply bend the material to their will but must work with them and accept they do not have total authorial control. This provides a model of material self-construction in which there is no single agency. But Bourgeois's work also give us insight into the nature of the materiality of self-construction, namely corporeality and its cultural iterations.

Ricoeur's narrative theory of the self advanced our understanding of the problem of self-construction. Following Ricoeur, I understand any unification of the self to be one that includes heterogenous elements, but I seek a model that can recognise that processes of self-construction are themselves multiple and diverse. Like Ricoeur, I am arguing that the self is constructed in a process of interpretation, but I want a better understanding of this interpretation as bodily than I believe the exemplar of literature can provide. I wish to maintain Ricoeur's nuanced insight into the circularity of a process in which self-construction impacts back on a cultural field which makes self-formation possible, but broaden our understanding of both the forms of self that are possible and the artistic activities that shape the field of practical action and meaning. It is to this end that I turn to other art practices.

NOTES

1. Meyers cites Merleau-Ponty's discussion of habit in *Phenomenology of Perception* in which he claims 'the phenomenon of habit in fact leads us to rework our notion of "understanding" and our notion of the body' (Merleau-Ponty 2012: 146).
2. Mackenzie and Meyers both draw on the work of Merleau-Ponty, though the debate between Mackenzie and Meyers includes a debate on the nuances and implications of Merleau-Ponty's account of bodily habit and expression (Mackenzie 2009; Meyers 2013).

3. A Corporeal Hermeneutics of the Self

INTRODUCTION

If we accept the importance of a self, which incorporates complexity, to our understanding of experience, and our future-orientated actions, yet reject the idea of a self that is simply given, we are faced with the question of how self-construction occurs. In Chapter 1, I argued that self-construction is a hermeneutic practice, which allows a multiplicity of experiences, drives and behaviours, etc., to contribute to the formation of a self, and can come to be interpreted as the experiences, drives and behaviours of a particular self. In the previous chapter, I explored the potential of narrative as a unifying interpretation that could effect this construction. I suggested that while it seemed well suited to understanding agency across time, providing an interpretation that connects past experience, present character and future actions, emplotment is only one interpretative activity among many that can contribute to producing and shaping a self. A self reduced to what can be incorporated into plot is therefore an impoverished self. For Ricoeur, any unification that produces a self is a unification that maintains heterogenous elements, but I seek a model that can adequately recognise that the processes of self-construction are themselves heterogenous. Once we expand our understanding of interpretation to include, as we have seen Nietzsche does, the evaluation and ascription of signification inherent in all actions and all the activity of drives, then we can understand a hermeneutics of the self to encompass practices as diverse as following a certain diet, the muscle memory of learning a skill, engaging in rituals of purification, or writing a diary, and to involve interpretations and desires that are not conscious.

Further, emplotment not only neglects the diversity of the hermeneutics of the self but fails to do justice to the corporeality of it. In my discussion of Goya's prints in the Introduction and of Bacon's paintings in the previous chapter, I emphasised the bodily character of our reactions to these artworks. Bacon's paintings speak to us on the level of sensation, as Deleuze would have it (2017), or to use Bacon's own term they act directly on the 'nervous-system' (Sylvester 1980: 18, 58–9). We have an immediate physical reaction when we encounter an image as disturbing and violent as *Three Studies for a Crucifixion* (1962). But, as I discussed in Chapter 2, it is not only that Bacon's paintings impact us physically, but that we identify with the bodies depicted, indeed this is part of why they impact us so strongly. We saw how Bacon's art makes us feel that we are flesh. While Ricoeur does not ignore that selves are embodied, he does not pay the body adequate attention. His theory of emplotment cannot adequately incorporate the plenitude of bodily activity that works to produce and shape a self. As discussed in the previous chapter, the body generates non-conceptual interpretations that cannot be expressed semantically or fitted into the mould of plot. Bodily activity is in excess of semantic capture. Therefore, while I am, like Ricoeur, arguing that the self is constructed through interpretation, I want a better understanding of these interpretations as bodily.

In developing a corporeal hermeneutics of the self, I wish to maintain Ricoeur's insight into the inherent circularity in the interaction between self-construction and the shaping of a shared cultural field in which this self-construction occurs. But I want to broaden our understanding of both the forms of self that are possible and the artistic activities that shape the field of action and meaning which support the creation of these forms. Corporeality is always expressed in the context of culture. That is, it is both interpreted in the context of culture and shaped by it. Drives for example adapt and express themselves in a way that a particular culture facilitates, as for instance in Nietzsche's account of the drive to cruelty turning inwards when society limits its direct expression (Nietzsche 2007: 57), while the body can be shaped, or disciplined, by various technologies, such as the effect of being under a continuous gaze as discussed in Foucault's analysis of the prison (Foucault 1995: 201). We still, however, need to recognise that both the cultural field and the self are shaped by and through the activity of the body, even if this activity is culturally mediated. While the latter claim is compatible with a narrative theory of the self, given that emplotment would then be construed as itself a bodily activity, once we start to pay attention to the body we become aware that emplotment can only incorporate a small part of the bodily activity that could contribute to our selfhood.

It is to this end, i.e. to develop a plural, corporeal hermeneutics of the self, that I turn to art practices beyond literature. The aim in this chapter is to elaborate an account of the hermeneutics of the self that can do justice to the diversity and corporeality of interpretative processes that can contribute to it, through a discussion of the work of Louise Bourgeois. By turning to the example of visual art I will offer a model of construction that can incorporate multiple, material processes in the creation of form, which we can then apply to the case of self-construction, to help describe how multiple, corporeal processes contribute to the creation of a self.

I will first discuss works by Bourgeois which explore the possibilities of material. Her art foregrounds the role of material as a condition of possibility but also as a constraint on the creation, and maintenance, of new forms by the artist. Through a discussion of artworks that are produced from stone, latex, wax, etc., we are able to explore the relationship between the creation of form and material processes. This will yield insights into this relationship which can subsequently be applied to our understanding of the relationship between selves and bodily processes. I will then discuss the nature of the materiality of self-construction in terms of corporeality, using works by Bourgeois which deepen our awareness and understanding of corporeality. This will involve emphasising the importance of process and the activity of drives. But we will also see how Bourgeois both asserts the eliminability of the body and testifies to the implications of the cultural context in which it is expressed and interpreted. Finally, I will consider how the understanding of the relationship between form-giving and material processes gained from a discussion of Bourgeois's early work can be applied as a model to help us understand the corporeality of self-construction. I will end by considering how Bourgeois herself has connected her artworks to her own self-construction, in terms of the continual work needed for her to maintain herself. In turning to a particular example of self-construction, namely the self-construction of Louise Bourgeois, I am not seeking to describe all cases of self-construction. In contrast to the model of emplotment, I am aiming to describe self-construction as inherently plural; there will thus be various ways that hermeneutic practices can combine in producing a self, and various possibilities for selfhood. But turning to examples of self-construction which demonstrate a diversity of simultaneous practices provides us with examples of what the model of emplotment excludes. Emplotment is thus shown to be too narrow an account of the hermeneutics of the self because it excludes modes of interpretation through which selves are and can be interpreted.

In discussing what we can learn from Bourgeois's work, I will draw on some of her own statements about her artwork, as well as insights from critics and art historians, and make connections between her artworks and some of her very personal writings. I believe that this can open up ways of seeing and learning from the work. But our encounter with the work itself, what we can find in it as viewers, is primary, and her own, or critics' interpretations are not treated as providing a final or exhaustive meaning.

THE ARTWORK AS WORKED MATTER

Visual art, or plastic art if the latter is broadly understood, whether paintings, sculptures, land art or performance art, involves an artist working on and through matter, such as paint, clay, earth or their own body. The artworks that are produced by the work of the artist, including sculptural forms, painted images or an interactive experience, depend on the material in and through which they are produced. Sculpture is the primary medium in which Louise Bourgeois works.[1] Many of Bourgeois's sculptures make clear to us the dependence of the artwork's form and meaning on the particular materials from which it is constructed, and the processes these materials undergo. We can thus deepen our understanding of the relationship between the production of form and material/material process through an engagement with her work, providing us with a model that can help us understand the relationship between the production of self and body/bodily processes. I will, therefore, start my discussion of Bourgeois's work by considering its materiality and what we can learn from it.

As Lucy Lippard observes, Bourgeois will make the same shape or explore the same theme in a variety of different materials:

> Throughout Bourgeois' oeuvre, shapes and ideas appear and disappear in a maze of versions, materials, incarnations. She has used latex as the soft avatar of her hard forms. A shape may be made first from soft plaster (which turns hard), then cast in latex so that a permanently soft mould, or skin, exists independently, then made in marble, which is the final epitome of hardness. (Lippard 1975: 30)

For example, *Avenza* (1968–9, Figure 3.1), a cluster of bulbous forms that seem to huddle together for protection, was made originally in plaster and subsequently cast in latex, bronze and plastic. The forms in *Avenza* take on different meanings depending on the material that produces them. The bronze version, *Avenza Revisited* (1968–9), which incorporated the plastic version, is visibly hard, the tops of the rounded protrusions shiny. It evokes the preservation of fossils; the potential of movement and growth suggested by the organic forms arrested by the bronze casting. Meanwhile the latex version, recast in 1992, has

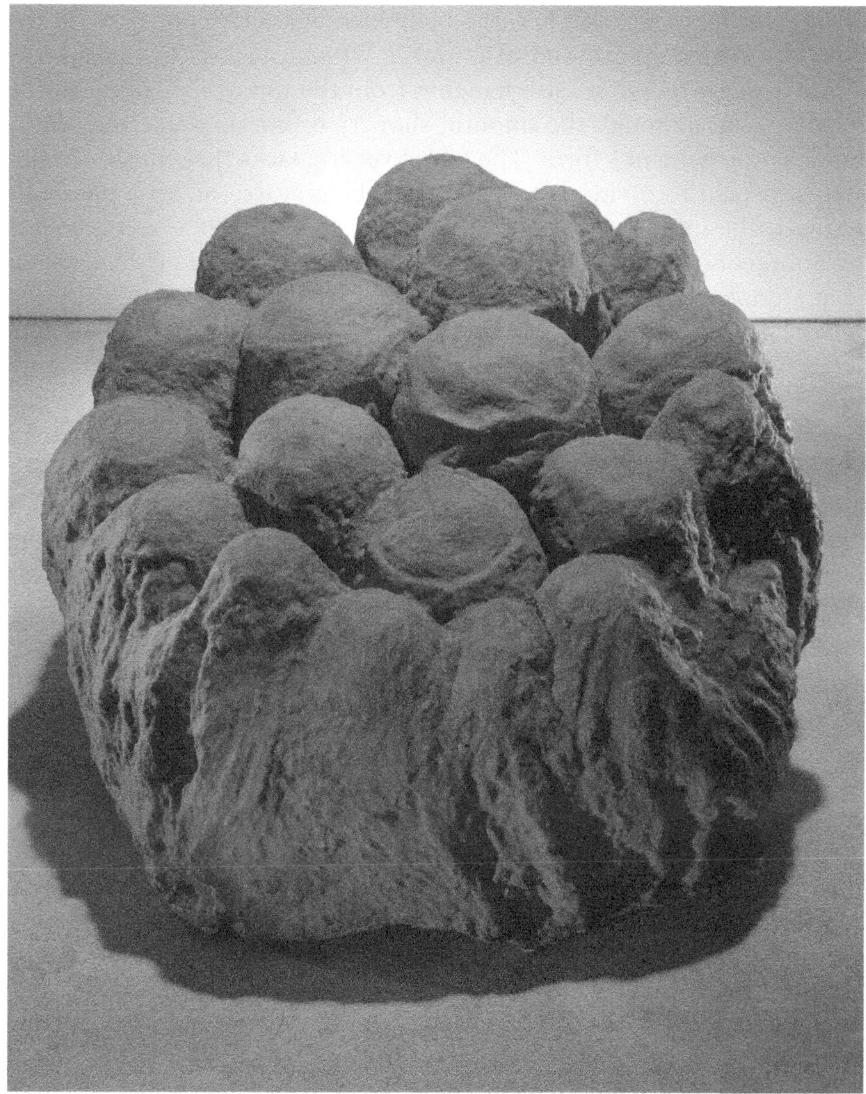

3.1 Louise Bourgeois, *Avenza*, 1968–9, latex and fibreglass, 53.3 × 76.2
× 116.8 cm. © The Easton Foundation/VAGA at ARS, NY and DACS, London
2020

a warmer feeling of shapes pressing together, and seems more alive, hinting at the possibility that they could continue to grow or multiply. Spirals are a shape, or pattern, that appear throughout Bourgeois's work, in both prints and sculptures. The latter include the bronze *Spiral Woman* (1984), a suspended figure, hanging lonely above a slate disc, whose arms, legs and (possibly pregnant) belly protrude from a spiral cocoon wrapped around her, the belly blending ambiguously with the final coil of the spiral, and also *Spiral Woman* (2003) in bluish grey cloth, armless this time, still hanging from the top of the spiral. In the former, it is as though the smooth, slippery bronze is squeezing out or birthing the woman's form. The fabric version lacks this movement but seems instead to invite us to poke into the crevasse or prise apart, or untwist, the muffling and insulating soft encasing. These experiments by Bourgeois thus demonstrate how the artwork's meaning depends on its material; material matters.

So, the significance of a particular artwork, the way that we will interpret its form, is influenced by its material properties. But more than that; the possibility of creating a particular form depends on the possibilities of the materials being worked on. In many of Bourgeois's pieces she explores and pushes to the limits the capacity of the materials she works with, but we shall see that her working of the material is also pushed towards the possibilities the materials contain. Following her wooden carvings and assemblages of the 1950s, she moved towards pliable materials including plaster and latex, revelling in their plasticity. Speaking to Robert Morgan in 1988 she claimed: 'Traditional materials limit where plaster, hot glue, rubber, latex, and plastic are the salt of pushing ahead into new concerns' (Morris 2007: 174). The forms which she creates from these experiments undulate, fold in on themselves, open out and confuse what is inside and outside. *Soft Landscape I* (1967) is one such example. Formed by pouring resin over shapes, it evokes both the corporeal and the geological. In gradations of brown, the overall shape rises up like a mountain, two gentle, rounded protrusions at the summit. The crevasse between them traces down into other lines and partial openings. The surface is wrinkled and dimpled, the softness that formed it is still tangible. It seems as though it would give way under your fingers if you pressed into it, though in fact the shape is long set.

Bourgeois is engaged in play with her materials, and she will often subvert our expectations of material properties. *Amoeba* (1963–5), a living blob of a sculpture, incipient life growing and pushing outwards, is made first in plaster, with its suitability to capture organic growth and movement due to its willingness to be moulded into new shapes. Yet this movement is arrested in the final sculpture which is cast in bronze. The white paint that covers the bronze evokes the cheaper and less durable plaster, but the resonance with a malleable material this creates is undercut by the hardness of the bronze beneath. Looking at *Amoeba*, it is as though a living creature is trapped beneath a hard epidermis or preserved in molten lava. In other sculptures, organic forms that evoke hills or breasts are captured in unyielding bronze or stone. For instance, consider the white marble *Blind Man's Bluff* (1984). This is a sculpture which mixes rough-cut, jagged shapes with smooth curves in polished marble. It consists of a stack of androgynous balls and protrusions, strongly suggestive of breasts, testicles and penises, but which could also be non-human growths, polyps or stalagmites. These shapes peep out from soft folds pulled taut, which might be the folds of cloth demonstrating the skills of the traditional statue maker, or the sensitive coverings of foreskin. The fine lines within the marble are like circulatory veins, suggesting bodily processes beneath the surface. The tower of shapes rests on a rough unpolished marble plinth and is topped by a jagged blade emerging from within its centre. The unpolished blade shows the cuts and marks of the sculptural process, the working on the material by the artist. Responding to this strange, confusing sculpture, Vincent Honoré pertinently suggests how 'the carnal protrusions contradict the cold hardness of the white marble' (Honoré 2007: 58). The carnal forms observed by Honoré set up a contrast with the blade that cuts through them. The hard properties of the marble facilitate the sculpting of the sharp edges of the blade, while I contend that we can understand the organic forms below as an experiment with the extent to which marble can successfully evoke the softness of the body despite its own hardness. The contrasting shapes thus give us the extremes of the material's capacity. Similarly, Anne Coxon claims that the series of sculptures *Soft Landscape* 'reflect the artist's interest in exploring the possibilities of her chosen materials, in particular the possibility that they could be used to disrupt the binary logic of "softness" and "hardness"' (Coxon 2007b: 272). This series depicts undulations, uprisings and layers using a variety of materials. When we consider the alabaster version of *Soft Landscape II* (1967), for instance, Coxon's comment seems apt. The sculpture offers us rounded, smooth shapes carved from hard material, which still appear vulnerable thanks to the stone's translucency. In Bourgeois's work we see how expectations of what we should do with a material, of the forms we expect from it, can be experimented with, pushed and disrupted, but materiality cannot be simply discarded.

If Bourgeois exploits the full potential of material, however, she is also acutely aware of its resistances. As she said in an interview with Robert Storr in 1986, regarding working with stone:

> You want a hole, it refuses to make a hole. You want it smooth, it breaks under the hammer. It is the stone that is aggressive. It is a constant source of refusal. You have to win the shape. It is a fight to the finish at every moment. (Bourgeois 1998: 142)

Pushing against the resistance of materials demonstrates how sculptural construction and formation are constrained and limited, as well as enabled, by materials. Hard wood or stone cannot be bent or twisted but only carved in imitation of bends and twists. There is a point at which materials will crack and fracture, and can be pushed no further.

Crucially, Bourgeois's exploration of material is an exploration of material processes. Resistances or limits, the point of fracture, are thus also to be understood in terms of material process. Commenting on her series *Soft Landscape* she writes:

> all the shapes have in common the fact that originally they were poured, and could only be obtained through that process. (The poured form is stretched from inside and obeys the laws of gravity.) For the pouring to be expressed you must have an elastic container. (Bourgeois 1998: 81)

To work with different materials, experimenting with the shapes they can produce, is to work with the processes of these materials; how they flow, expand, shrink, harden, melt, dry, crack, and so on. For example, her experiments include 'placing wet wood inside plaster; the plaster dried the wood, which then split its shell' (Lippard 1975: 31). Materials, however, can lose their plasticity. There is a stress limit before which some materials will shatter, and a time limit during which certain materials remain pliable before they harden or dry out. In her diary from 1994, Bourgeois writes about working in clay: 'When the water evaporates fragmentation takes place. Fissures everywhere, clay, regular inert clay. An adhesive is needed. I become obsessed with the need for binder or adhesive' (Morris 2007: 174). The activity of the material, its tendencies and vicissitudes, thus shape the sculptor's activity.

Thus, to produce a sculpture Bourgeois must work matter but the matter is not inert, and as sculptor she does not have total control of the material processes, such as melting, evaporating, hardening, etc., that contribute to the final form. It is not just a question of the resistances that the artist meets in working the material, a refusal to be shaped, but also that there are alternative processes of shaping that elude the artist's control, a refusal to remain in one shape. Through sculpture, Bourgeois makes the multiplicity of processes, and the impossibility of total authorial control, visible and tangible to the viewer. The material processes that contribute to her sculptural works continue without the specific intervention and direction of the artist as agent; the material pushes ahead. Latex is malleable for the artist but, as Coxon notes in her discussion of *Avenza* (1968–9, Figure 3.1), it is also unpredictable (2007a: 52). The sculptor can unite different material processes in one work, giving the work an overall form, which employs this heterogeneity, but the processes are activities themselves, or have their own 'lives', which also shape this form and elude the artist's control.

The recognition of the activity of the material which Bourgeois's work demands is a crucial insight that we need to apply to the case of self-construction. The various processes that contribute to the hermeneutics of the self are not under the control of an author. Material processes push forward according to their own trajectories. The capacity of visual art to work with these trajectories and incorporate what does not fit the mould (or perhaps its incapacity to entirely exclude it?) is precisely why it offers an effective model for a corporeal hermeneutics of the self. Bourgeois succeeds in her work in including excess and multiple processes. For instance, '[s]he made works from what are normally the remnants of the casting process, combining them in new ways and presenting what is negative as positive' (Coxon 2010: 41). This is precisely what the template of plot cannot do, it does not allow a way to present what cannot be plotted. Plot can inherently incorporate change and development across time, and there is variety within what constitutes a plot and a narrative structure, but this variety is limited. Literature can experiment with different forms, but this involves alternatives to narrative. Hence, for Ricoeur, given that the self for him is a narrative self, the breakdown of character (and thus self) which we see in *The Man Without Qualities* is concomitant with the breakdown of plot. What cannot be incorporated in the process of emplotment cannot be part of a narrative self. Plot thus restricts the self.

A corporeal hermeneutics of the self that seeks inspiration from visual art can embrace a plurality of processes, which push forward with their own, sometimes contradictory, concerns. For example, as I will discuss below, for Bourgeois's own hermeneutics of the self this includes the physicality of her own art making. A hermeneutics of the self may also incorporate, as I will discuss in relation to Cindy Sherman's work in Chapter 4, the way that we impose identities on others in response to visual cues. A hermeneutics of the self might encompass the internalisation of an objectifying or constantly monitoring gaze, the deliberate conditioning of the body in an attempt to meet an ideal, the expression of libidinal drives, the restrictions placed on physical activity by pollution-damaged lungs. It allows for the multiplicity of interpretative processes that have their own material imperatives, just as Bourgeois's sculptures work with the various material processes that push the form in different directions.

In looking at Bourgeois's work, we are not only made aware of the multiplicity of processes involved in the production of the work, but also that they are never final or permanent. The biomorphic works are incomplete, suggesting to us the possibility of further growth or change. In *Avenza Revisited II* (1968–9), the bulbous protrusions are not cradling each other as in *Avenza* (1968–9, Figure 3.1), but ambiguously seem to either grow out of or be flowing away into the structure of strands beneath it, which pool in coils on the wooden plinth on which the plastic and plaster shape rests. The *Cumul* and *Avenza* series both strike me with a sense of fecundity, suggesting the potential for reproductive multiplication. In addition to the openness of form, with the suggestion of future development and reproduction, the potential of disintegration and degradation underscore for the viewer that no form is ever fixed or permanent. The latex which Bourgeois found so amenable to her sculptural experiments degrades over time, losing its shape when exposed to light and heat. The bulbous growths of *Cumul I* (1969) could multiply as I suggested above, or alternatively melt away like the cloud formations the sculpture is named after. Where complex processes are woven together, they could pull apart. When discussing her later *Cells*, which she introduces in 1989, in which different sculptural elements and objects are brought together in various enclosures, Bourgeois speaks of 'an urge to integrate, merge, or disintegrate' (Bourgeois 1998: 205). This description, and the sense of process in many of her works, resonates with a note in Nietzsche's unpublished *Nachlass* where he writes 'the original tendency of protoplasm in sending out pseudopodia and feeling its way. Assimilation and incorporation is, above all, a willing to overwhelm [. . .] If this incorporation fails, the formation will probably fall apart' (1988: vol. 12, 424). Some of Bourgeois's works evoke simple life forms, such as the protoplasm Nietzsche is discussing here, and illustrate the inherent tendency of all life to expand, grow and merge but also to disintegrate and separate.

Both the impermanence implied by the nature of any processes, which can continue or regress, and the tensions of holding together multiple processes indicate a struggle between form and formlessness. Bourgeois's many spiral forms for instance seem poised to unravel. In *Clutching* (1962), in which a small anthropomorphic figure holds onto and is held by a sinuous twist of strands, the sculpture is tangibly holding itself together. As Coxon writes of Bourgeois's spiral forms there is 'always a sense that the strung-up, wrung-out shape could unravel, releasing the tension and spiralling out of control at any moment' (Coxon 2010: 41). The creation of form is thus tenuous and temporary. In Bourgeois's work, Lippard rightly stresses: 'form and the formless are locked in constant combat' (Lippard 1975: 33). Hence, form requires work to create it and to maintain it.

What lessons have we gained from this discussion of the relationship between form and material in Bourgeois's work? We have seen how the possibilities of the work's form depend on the possibilities of the material, and the final form and its meaning are not separable from the material it is made in. The artist can experiment and push these possibilities, but resistances will be met, and materials will push the artwork in new directions. There are multiple processes which can contribute to the form which escape the control of the artist, and the inherent continuations, regressions and interactions of material processes imply that forms are temporary and changeable, requiring work and maintenance. Before we can apply this model to a discussion of self-construction, however, we need to consider further the nature of the material/material processes that self-construction in particular involves.

CORPOREALITY

We have seen in previous chapters how our reactions to artworks include physical disturbances and excitements, often including a sense of identification with the bodies or flesh portrayed. Artists such as Goya and Bacon give us an experience of our corporeality. In the previous chapter, I argued that as a visual artist Bacon adds to an exploration and experience of loss of self, such as we might also find in some modernist literature, a physical awareness that the self has a bodily vulnerability. Self and body are thus inextricably entangled and a hermeneutics of the self needs to recognise this. My contention is that once we pay attention to our corporeality, we will recognise the diversity of processes that can contribute to self-construction and see that emplotment is a restricted account of a hermeneutics of the self. Bourgeois's art can help with this task of paying attention to and understanding the nature of this corporeality. She claims of her own work that:

> Content is a concern with the human body, its aspects, its changes, transformations, what it needs, wants and feels – its functions.
> What it perceives and undergoes passively, what it performs.
> What it feels and what protects it – its habitat.
> (Bourgeois 1998: 76)

This claim, that her work is concerned with the human body, is borne out by an examination of her oeuvre. Many of her sculptures, with their sacs, protrusions and lumps, are biomorphic. While some have a general biomorphic character, others are clearly evocative of the human body and in particular its sexual and reproductive characteristics. We see breasts, penises, testicles, pregnant bellies and umbilical cords. The sea of shapes in *Cumul I* (1969) is one obvious example, ambiguous between landscape, animal and human body it manifests corporeality at the level of the cellular, or simple organisms, but also suggests sexual organs. Rosalind Krauss observes how 'the choice of sculptural medium – rubber latex, plastic, plaster, wax, resin, hemp – is consistently pushed towards the evocation of bodily organs' (Krauss 2000: 55).

It is not just the shapes they enable but the texture and colour of many of Bourgeois's chosen materials that have a bodily character. The presence, and vulnerability, of flesh can be seen in the early use of latex and the later use of fabric, particularly with the choice of pink cloth. *Destruction of the Father* (1974) is a sculpture of a dismembered body, innards exposed and partly devoured, the red lighting adding to the latex's plasticity in depicting a tableaux of mutilated flesh. *Destruction of the Father* is an extreme example of flesh, exposing the inside of a body, but in other works our fleshiness is also apparent under the covering of skin. Lippard observes the significance of skin in Bourgeois's early work:

> Like many women, she identifies surfaces with her skin – it can be the cloth in Cumulous, or a thin layer of peeling latex over bulbous plaster, or the heavier folds in Fillette, or a glowing flow of dark resin totally immersing underlying forms. (Lippard 1975: 33)

It is with the fabric work that the skin's vulnerability, as something tenuously holding together, protective but porous and capable of being wounded, comes across most. This resonates particularly when Bourgeois selects pink tones. Coxon describes these 'fleshy pink soft sculptures', noting how for the viewer 'the gaps in the stitching and roughly patched-up areas are a reminder of the porous quality of our own skin and the delicacy of flesh that may succumb to sickness or trauma' (Coxon 2010: 81). Examples of Bourgeois's cloth, doll-like personages, include *Do Not Abandon Me* (1999), *Seven in Bed* (2001), *Fragile Goddess* (2002) and *Three Horizontals* (1998). As its name suggests, *Three Horizontals* comprises three figures, they are displayed on a metal frame reminiscent of a mortuary trolley, one on top of the other. The upper figure is torn and exposed. This is a wounded body, clearly vulnerable to injury in the way that Coxon has observed. The middle figure is smaller, childlike but still feminine. The bottom figure appears amputated, consisting of breasts and truncated limbs. They are, I suggested above, doll-like, but these are dolls of flesh, not cold porcelain nor hard plastic. Capable of being dismembered, they have *content*, innards. Even when working in the hard whiteness of marble Bourgeois suggests the covering of skin, as with *Blind Man's Bluff* (1984). Skin, a membrane that can be pierced, implies the presence of activity beneath it. This bodily content, held together by skin, is what Bourgeois claims, in the quote above, is the content of her art. The quote continues thus:

> All these states of being, perceiving and doing are expressed by processes that are familiar to us and that have to do with the treatment of materials, pouring, flowing, dripping, oozing out, setting, hardening, coagulating, thawing, expanding, contracting, and the voluntary aspects such as slipping away, advancing, collecting, letting go – (Bourgeois 1998: 76)

If the human body, the content which Bourgeois attributes to her own work, is expressed through these various material processes, this suggests that for Bourgeois the body is a body of processes: digestion, breathing, division, reproduction, secretion, bleeding. Her work reminds us that the body is not a static figure. She makes us aware of bodily processes with some pieces hinting at cells multiplying or the results of defecation, and others explicitly addressing sex, pregnancy and nursing. For example, the kneeling breastfeeding mother, fashioned in pink fabric, that forms part of the tableaux *Oedipus* (2003) captures the intimacy of breastfeeding perfectly in the soft placement of the baby's arm on its mother's breast. Thus, engaging with Bourgeois's art reminds us that the body undergoes constant processes and 'transformations', just as the materials of her sculptures do.

So, Bourgeois's work renders tangible the process character of the body. But she also reminds us that bodies have 'needs' and 'feel'. How do we understand such needs and feelings in terms of bodily process? The idea that bodily processes include the interpretative activity of bodily drives, and that we can understand wants, needs and feelings in terms of drives, is a theory common to both Nietzsche and Freud, on which I elaborated in Chapter 1. The interpretation of drives explains the complexity and the physicality of our experience of art. Artworks provide evidence for the theory of drives. How do artworks help us understand the nature of the drives? One level on which artworks can deepen our understanding of drives is by engaging the drives of the viewer and making them aware of drive activity. This is something that I explored in the Introduction in relation to Goya; we respond to *The Disasters of War* prints in complex – sometimes contradictory – ways, suggesting different drives which are stimulated by and interpret and evaluate the images variously. By reflecting on our experience of the artwork we become aware of the complexity and activity of drives. The experience of engaging with the artwork also affects this activity, and thus acts on the body, a possibility to which I will return in the next section of this chapter.

We can also view artworks as the result of the form-giving capacity of drives and thus as providing insight into their form-giving potential. As Bourgeois suggests '[s]culpture can integrate many a blind and shapeless aggression' (2012: 128–9). Mignon Nixon notes how Bourgeois came to sculpture via engraving, adapting 'gouging, digging and incising', all potentially expressions of violence (2005: 167). At the end of a passage in Bourgeois's notes where she writes about the anomaly of a broken mother comes the line 'the clay is my mother April 27-57 forms *eye socket*' (Bourgeois 2012: 54). We can envisage fingers violently digging into the soft clay. Clay can be gouged and attacked, but also caressed and smoothed. Through these processes, both aggressive and libidinal drives find some release, but they are themselves also reshaped to allow for new unities and coherences.

These unities, the form given to the artwork, have their own meaning as a distinct forms. But they are not isolated. Both making and engaging with art can be understood as a continuation of bodily activity. Jerry Gorovoy, Bourgeois's long-time studio assistant, reported in conversation with Deborah Wye that 'She'd say "Oh, my work is my body."' Gorovoy said that he saw 'the work almost as fibrillation of a Heartbeat. It's almost like the forms are coming out of her body' (Wye 2017: 199). Body understood as processes – heartbeats, secretions, the attractions and agitations of drives – extends beyond any particular physical structure of bone and flesh. Louise Bourgeois's work can thus be viewed as an extension of her body and part of her self-construction, questioning the rigidity of any boundaries we would place around a body or a self.

The drives which Bourgeois's works provide insight into can be understood as both bodily and as always both interpreted and themselves interpreting in a cultural context. This does not mean that culture can mould them indiscriminately, but rather that drives must adapt to the context in which they operate, as in the example mentioned in Chapter 1 of the drives turning inwards in their expression to establish a 'bad conscience' (Nietzsche 2007: 57). The form they take is thus shaped by this context. The society in which we live also both frames our expectations of bodies and further works to actually shape our bodies and types of bodies. Bourgeois's series of works, *Femme Maison*, is a potent reminder of the former. The title plays on house woman and housewife, perhaps also suggesting *femme fatale* (Nixon 2005: 53), and it explores the expectations placed on women, and their bodies. In various drawings and sculptures by Bourgeois, we see women with heads, and sometimes torsos, encased in houses. For instance, *Femme Maison* (1994) in white marble, depicts a reclining naked woman with her head inside a stylised house, reminiscent of a child's wooden toy. Her naked body is exposed and vulnerable. The house, domesticity, traps her but fails to shelter and protect her. Her body remains public, a commodified means of reproduction. Her role is to remain in the house but to be available to become impregnated and bear children. These social demands provide the context in which bodies are interpreted. At the same time, they provide the context in which bodies interpret and shape themselves. Various bodily activities and processes, from breathing, eating, copulating, running or sitting, including the interpretations and expressions of bodily drives, contribute to shaping particular bodies, associated with particular selves. So, corporeality is engaged in interactive processes of shaping and being shaped by cultural practices. The material of our self-construction is thus corporeality, the activity of the body and bodily drives, in its cultural manifestations. The preceding discussion of Bourgeois's work highlights the multiplicity and continual activity of the body, including the activity of drives, but also that this activity occurs in a cultural context which influences this activity. What though does it mean to say that various bodily processes, including drives, as they manifest in a cultural context, are what construct the self?

CORPOREALITY OF SELF-CONSTRUCTION

Let us remind ourselves what is at stake in self-construction. In order to be able to talk about a self, with a past and future, who experiences tensions and contradictions, we have to interpret actions across time, diverse feelings and multiple bodily processes as those of a particular self. My argument is that diverse and sometimes unconscious processes contribute to the continual production of such selves making possible this interpretation. However, to posit the interpretative activity of drives, and diverse bodily processes, as driving the construction of a self can be viewed as presenting a problem of agency. However, this problematic can be altered when we consider what we mean by agency. When we attribute agency to a particular self, we assume this involves self-awareness; in explaining why a given self acts a certain way we appeal to motivations and intentions in connection to an idea we have of our own character, plans and projects. This is a thick concept of agency, the agency of a conscious self that can reflect on itself. If we are looking, rather, for an explanation of the forces which can contribute to and drive self-construction, then what we have is not a lack of agency but an excess. Unless we presume that all agency must be conscious, or that it must be stable, we can view the drives, and automatic processes, such as fibrillation and peristalsis, as shifting loci of agential direction which assert various interpretations and pursue various goals in ways that will shape a particular self. Once a self emerges from these processes, and we come to have a sense of ourselves as selves, we may then consciously choose to work on or shape ourselves in line with a particular ideal, but we will not have total control over the self that is produced as there will continue to be unconscious processes, drives asserting their interpretations or pushing us to act in ways which we are not aware of, power strategies of others and various by-products of behaviours and practices.

Our discussion of Bourgeois's work has helped emphasise that there are a myriad of bodily processes, including drive activity, that can contribute to a hermeneutics of the self in which particular selves are produced. Further, her work supports the view that body is expressed and moulded in the context of a shared culture, by illustrating ways in which this occurs. Let us now return to what we learnt by examining the relation between the construction of form and material processes in Bourgeois's artworks earlier in this chapter, to see how this applies to the relation between the construction of the self and corporeal processes.

The first point that we drew out by examining Bourgeois's work is that the form the artist is able to give to an artwork depends on the possibilities of the materials on and through which they work. Similarly, any self that is formed depends on the possibilities of our corporeality. But we also saw that the artist can play with and experiment with the possibilities of material. How does such play occur in relation to our corporeality? This can be through working directly on and with the body as many performance artists do. Where the body is used as the material of the artwork, as in the artist ORLAN's surgeries in *Re-incarnation of Saint ORLAN* (beginning 1990), muscle, skin, flesh and cartilage are themselves pushed to the limits of their plasticity. Working on the body is not the sole purview of artists, however. On Foucault's analysis the body is continually disciplined in contemporary society, in for instance processes of medical and educational examination. While his analysis in *Discipline and Punish* (Foucault 1995) focuses on the operation of power on us, according to strategies of control, we can include work on the body as part of the understanding of 'technologies of the self' that Foucault explores subsequently (Foucault 1988). These technologies can, as I will consider in the next chapter, work to enforce norms and produce subjugated subjects. They can also, however, be taken up in creative ways and thus be part of experimenting with the body and its capacities.

But I have argued above that the material of self-construction is not naked corporeality, but bodies, and the activity of bodily drives, as they are expressed and shaped culturally. And this cultural articulation of the body can be played with in works made in mediums other than flesh. Bourgeois mischievously delights in such play. We can see this in her distortion of male and female sexual organs, for instance in *Janus Fleuri* (1968) and *Fillette* (1968). The former casts two mirror-image phallic shapes in bronze, the centre suggesting female genitalia, while *Fillette*, combining latex and plaster, is most simply described as an oversized penis suspended from the ceiling, though it can also be seen as a female torso, showing how one shape can take on different significations. Bourgeois thus rejects, and playfully confuses, expectations of binary gender. *Fillette* (1968) is perhaps the most obvious example of this, collapsing as it does the opposition between male and female: '*Fillette* acts to blur this distinction as the vaginal opening at the foot of the shaft and between the two testicles forces male and female to merge' (Krauss 2007: 146). It is at once a male penis and a female torso, the balls at the bottom playing the role of either testicles or hip joints. Another sexually ambiguous piece is *Fragile Goddess* (2002), a pink felt, female torso with full breasts and rounded pregnant belly, sprouting a phallic shape from her neck in place of a head. This work represents the pregnant woman as possessing, and being partly shaped by, aggressive, stereotypically 'male' drives. Hence, Bourgeois's work gives us a model for how a self-construction operating with the material of a corporeality that is already interpreted and shaped in a cultural context does not have to passively accept these interpretations but can challenge, play and reinterpret this material.

The use of visual art brings together the activity of working on the cultural body and working on individual bodies. Artworks can challenge, subvert, appropriate and reinvent cultural representations of the body and culturally acceptable forms of drive expression and at the same time have an effect on the bodies of the audience who engage with them. If we remember the effect that Goya and Bacon have on us, we can see how our engagement with visual art can be physically persuasive, can actually affect our drives and our bodies. Artworks can make us recoil, they can agitate us to action. In engaging the drives, they participate in the development of the drives. In both these senses visual artworks can be technologies of the self. They can, as representations of the body and expressions of drives, critique and experiment with the cultural articulation of corporeality. They can also engage the drives and move the body, and as such they are part of the moulding of this body.

So, turning to the relationship between form and material in visual

artwork provides us with a model of how we can play with the possibilities of material in self-construction, and these visual artworks can
also provide us with a means for such play, as I will consider further in
Chapter 5. But while we can play with the material of bodies, and their
cultural representations and expressions, just as the stone will offer
resistance to the artist who strives to carve it, we will meet resistances
from corporeality. The example of Bourgeois's sculptures underscores
for us that material makes possible but also limits.

As well as providing a model of construction that emphasises
the potential of materials to resist the imposition of form, some of
Bourgeois's works provide insight into the particular resistance that
the material of self-construction presents us. Bourgeois demonstrates
the stone-like challenge of culturally mediated corporeality faced by
women in their attempts to shape themselves. She confronts ideas of
gender in general and expectations around reproduction in particular
in her work. In the series of *Femme Maison* works discussed above, it is
clear that the refuge of social conformity is a prison not a haven.

In her notes, Bourgeois writes the following powerful passage:

> of course the warm palm which is a mother can be a bad one. An inad-
> equate or *degenerate* mother > < obviously terror sets in – a Broken mother
> is like a cold house – or a soft walking stick or a *rotten plank – it is an
> anomaly.* Paulson story about the bombed out bomb shelter where the
> shelter becomes a trap – the "good mother" becomes a trap a slogan a catch
> word to use against you or seduce you with literally a devil a wolf in sheep's
> clothing and it turns you the poor +silly sheep into a revengeful world. The
> birth of violence could be the title of these lines- heart beats come again *hat
> of acorn* pig in the blanket – the clay is my mother April 27-57 forms *eye
> socket* (Bourgeois 2012: 54)

Here, not only do social and cultural expectations of the body provide
constraints on interpretations of selves and the identities that a self
incorporates, such as woman, mother, wife, child, but we also see how
the process of self-construction can be one in which plasticity is lost;
just as Bourgeois's sculpting was frustrated by clay drying out, we
can become petrified within a particular identity. The role of a good
mother operates both as an impossible standard and as a trap. As
Bourgeois recounts of one of her dreams, there is both pride and terror
in motherhood:

> I have this little baby
> *I am very proud of it it is godsend
> Yvonne is jealous people appreciate me
> a whole army is here with the King and
> the queen reviewing the troops.*

Here I am breast-feeding the child
and people look at me
waiting and the orchestra even stops
playing.
the child has grown, he needs to be changed he urinates in a blanket and it
makes me hysterical *I run around.*
(Bourgeois 2012: 147)

Connecting this account of her dream and the earlier passage, with the idea of the 'trap of the good mother', conveys the powerful fear of being a broken mother, of the body not functioning as it is expected, of not being enough. The mould of good mother and good wife cannot accommodate anxiety, dissatisfaction or even, as with the defensive protrusions in the series of *Fragile Goddess* works, maternal aggression, the latter, as Nixon notes, remains taboo (Nixon 2005: 152). Indeed, neither can the mould of loving and devoted daughter accommodate the fear and resentment that such dependence can induce, alongside love and gratitude. If these drives and feelings are excluded from our self-understanding as a mother (or daughter) then constructing ourselves in a way that incorporates the identify of being a mother (or daughter) involves denying or expunging these elements. The subsumption of the woman to her pregnancy is one possible reading of the *Spiral Woman* figures; only the belly, legs and sometimes arms left visible. The encased upper bodies suggest the possibility of suffocation of aspects of the self in the maternal role.

The notion that identity can be a trap, suggested by Bourgeois's discussions here resonates with Foucault's concern that we can be tied to our identities in a way that supports contemporary power regimes, a theme I will return to in the next chapter (Foucault 1982: 781). Bourgeois's artistic explorations of these difficult themes and portrayals of women and mothers can contribute to the self-construction of her audience, by exposing how gender roles and social expectations can function as a trap, and revealing the suffering that trying to confine oneself to such a mould, and to deny alternative drive interpretations, produces. Such criticisms can open up space for alternative interpretations of self and alternative expressions of drives. The *Femme Maison* series is an indictment of the domestic sphere as alleged safe haven. As such it helps women to break free of this ideal of what it is to be a female self and interpret themselves and their desires differently. The important role of visual artworks in this process of critique will be discussed in more detail in Chapter 4.

But some of Bourgeois's artworks on the subject of pregnancy and motherhood succeed in incorporating elements that do not fit this mould of the 'good mother' and thus model the possibility of a self-construction that can incorporate diverse and ambivalent interpretations, including interpretations that existing templates of selfhood would exclude. Her work both reveals the resistance that social and cultural expectations of our bodies and roles present to self-construction and asserts the importance of what is excess of social moulds, and the possibility of expanding our understanding of self-construction to allow for this complexity and ambivalence. Bourgeois made four sculptures with the title *The Woven Child* in 2002. One is a fabric and thread work which presents a pregnant torso and foetus, heartbreakingly fragile in its delicate net (Figure 3.2). There is an immense sense of tenderness in the sculpture, the unborn child cocooned in blue mesh is a beautiful image. But headless and limbless, the women's body is given over entirely to this pregnancy, she offers an image which celebrates fertility with her pregnant belly and full breasts, but she is also helpless. In another of these sculptures bearing the same name, another fabric and thread torso has breasts and belly highlighted with red circles while the baby rests against the mother's body, head buried in her bosom. The soft figure of the child caresses its mother, but this is a mother who is armless and cannot clutch her child to her breast. These fabric mother and child pairs capture a sense of maternal love but are also expressive of isolation and inadequacy. This capacity to incorporate tensions and capture ambivalence is present in what is perhaps Bourgeois's best-known work, *Maman* (1999). This giant spider, elegant and domineering, expresses love and admiration, but an immense spider, while reparative, is also menacing. As Gorovoy says in his 2017 interview with Wye: 'There were always conflicting emotions contained within the same motif' (Wye 2017: 198). This is clearly the case in the repeated use of spiders: 'the spider both protects and imprisons' (Wye 2017: 174). The spider's capacity for mending its web connects to Bourgeois's mother's work as a tapestry restorer, but the web is also something that catches us and prevents our escape.

These diverse works connect to powerful and ambivalent feelings of motherhood, the desire for it, fear of it and conflicted experiences of it, and to the complexity in our relationships to our mothers. They, therefore, engage a range of bodily drives, and express a range of drive interpretations. Many of Bourgeois's artworks capture ambivalence. In doing so they incorporate the different interpretations of different drives into one work. Bourgeois's works thereby provide concordant discordance within a given moment, holding together more than one perspective and more than one conflicting need and its interpretations together, without letting any of them subsume the others or rip apart the form, though the danger of this disintegration often remains palpable.

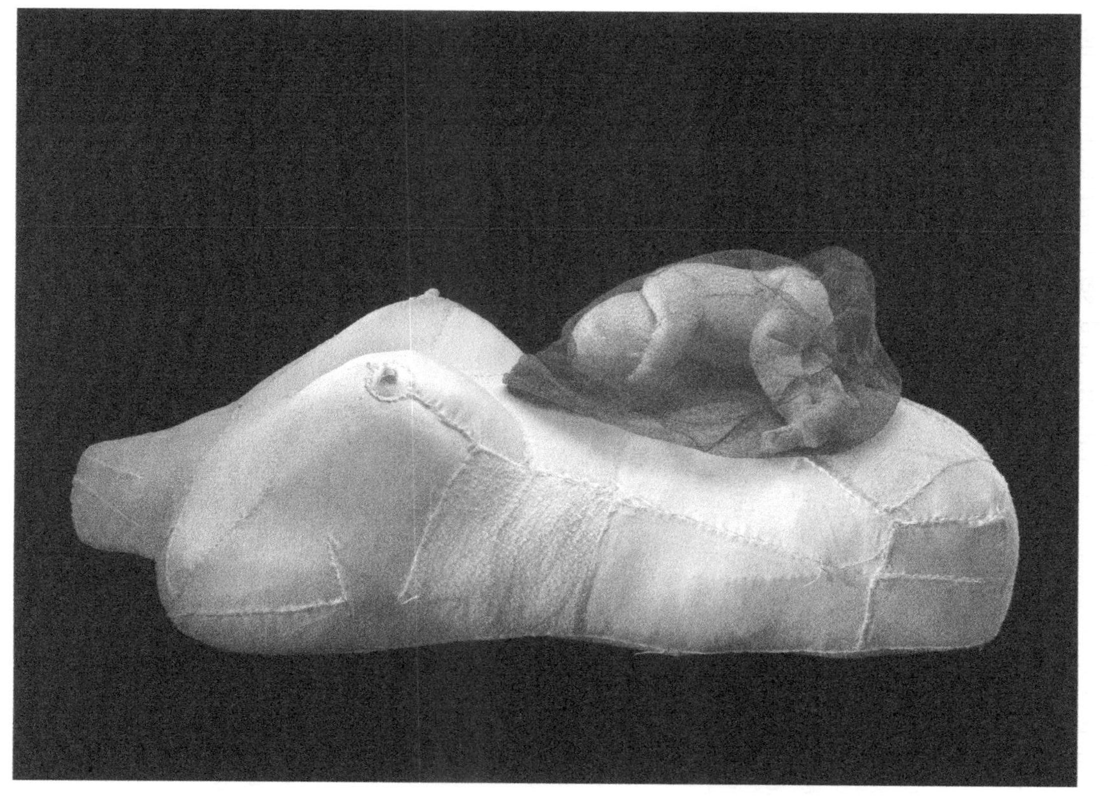

3.2 Louise Bourgeois, *The Woven Child*, 2002, fabric and thread, 27.9 × 73.7 × 36.8 cm. © The Easton Foundation/VAGA at ARS, NY and DACS, London 2020

From the discussion of Louise Bourgeois's sculpting we learn that it is not just direct refusal, and petrification, of material that limits how an artist can work matter but also slippage, excess, the material's own vicissitudes. We can again extend these insights concerning the relationship between form and material process to self-construction. Corporeal processes elude our control, and self-construction is not something we can take complete control of. In an interview with Paul Herkenhoff, Bourgeois says: 'We are as malleable as wax. Descartes talked about wax. We talk of a ball of wax. Therefore, we are sensitive to the memory of what happened before and [sensitive] to the apprehension of what will happen' (Morris 2007: 174). This assertion of the self's plasticity clearly frames self-construction as open to change and even reconstruction. But it also suggests that this malleability implies a vulnerability. Our self-construction interacts with our environment, and the corporeal processes that form us are literally impressionable. Events, experiences, relationships all leave imprints on us, influencing the particular way drives develop and particular bodies take shape, just as a fingerprint does in wax; affecting the form the wax takes. Our diet, our posture, our exercise regime all make impressions on our body and its drives. But so do our relationships, our experiences and our traumas.

We saw with the example of sculpture that the material processes of construction through which form is given can regress and unravel. When we connect this to self-construction this suggests the need to maintain and continually work on the self. To construct and sustain a self involves holding conflicting elements together and incorporating change without being overwhelmed and subsumed.

It is here that the personal aspects of Bourgeois's work are pertinent to our discussion. Her artwork can be read as a kind of self-work or therapy, holding off a disintegration of the self which she felt threatened her. Lucy Lippard connects her observations about the struggle to find form in Bourgeois's work with Bourgeois herself:

> Within the art (as, one suspects, within the artist) form and the formless are locked in constant combat. The outcome is an unusually exposed demonstration of the intimate bond between art and its maker. Despite her apparent fragility, Bourgeois is an artist, and a woman artist, who has survived almost 40 years of discrimination, struggle, intermittent success and neglect, in New York's gladiatorial art arenas. The tensions which make her work unique are forged between just those poles of tenacity and vulnerability. (Lippard 1975: 33)

While Nixon suggests the struggle of maintaining a coherent self is palpable in Bourgeois's artworks:

Bourgeois' art is, from the beginning, in solidarity with the struggle for psychic integration and adaptation to reality.

But it also seems deeply sceptical – or phantasically realistic – about the possibility of their attainment. (Nixon 2005: 112)[2]

Both critics are sensitive to the struggle that Bourgeois faces in her own self-construction. Lippard draws attention to the social and cultural resistances which Bourgeois faced in trying to establish herself as an artist in a male-dominated world. But Nixon is aware of the underlying challenge for Bourgeois of maintaining and giving coherence to difficult drives. We do not have to accept the Freudian story regarding the circumstances of repression and the particular content of the drives that now seek to return and express themselves[3] in order to view Bourgeois's work as involving getting her drives in control, holding herself together and working through her own difficult feelings. Writing in her private notebooks of her 'strong impulse to "make a figure usual Size 5½ feet"', she suggests: 'This figure I feel pushed to make is going to dissolve or appease my anxiety' (Bourgeois 2012: 42). Her continual diary-keeping included writing, tape-recording and, most importantly by her own admission, drawing. These processes of recording were, she said, ways for her to 'keep my house in order. They must be up-to-date so that I'm sure life does not pass me by' (Herkenhoff 2007: 104). This task was continual. For Bourgeois there is a palpable threat that her drives might overwhelm the emergence of nascent forms of selfhood, and any unification turn to disintegration. Repairing herself, holding herself together, and in Nietzsche's terms getting control of her 'drives and their for and against' (Nietzsche 1988: vol. 12, 315) required her continual artistic activity. The process of making is crucial to Bourgeois's self-management; providing ways of expressing and working through impulses that might otherwise take a destructive form. In Louise Bourgeois's case art making is a technology of the self that enables her to integrate tensions and work through anxieties. For her, then, her work itself forms part of her self-construction. The hermeneutics of the self in the case of Bourgeois herself involves sculpting, drawing, assembling as much as narrating. In looking at Bourgeois's art as a hermeneutic activity that contributes to her producing and maintaining herself, we see that, and how, self-construction involves multiple and corporeal activities, but we cannot hope to find a one-size-fits-all mould for selves. Nor do I think such a template is desirable, and I will suggest in Chapter 4 that the attempt to present a precisely delineated account of how we become selves is potentially oppressive and limiting of selfhood, excluding what cannot be incorporated into a particular mould.

The above discussion has underscored the importance of paying attention to bodily processes and drives in our exploration of how selves are and can be constructed. The comparison with visual artworks has also served to draw out the implications of recognising the corporeality of our hermeneutics of the self, requiring that we acknowledge the resistances, refusal to be tamed and reversibility of the diverse processes that contribute to shaping us. The example of visual and plastic artworks also illustrates how such diverse corporeal processes can interact in and be incorporated into the construction of a particular self.

CONCLUSION

A narrative account of self-construction aims to account for continuity of a self across time. Can an account of self-construction drawn from diverse visual art practices address this problem too? Visual artworks do not take the same temporal form as the novel, but they are not static either, they emerge from various processes and may regress or disintegrate. It would be a false dichotomy to set up non-literary arts as an entirely non-temporal contrast to literature. We can see in Bourgeois's sculptures marks of these processes such as drips, swirls, cracks, imprints from moulds; all are intimations of the transient nature of any form. Understanding self-construction in terms of the relationship between form and material that we see in visual art making does not, therefore, entirely lack the temporal aspect of the novel. The analogy of visual art shows us that self-construction is ongoing, that form and formlessness are always in tension. Considering Bourgeois's work illustrates how multiple processes that occur simultaneously can unify, but this unification depends on development and interactions that play out in time and is not a question of a final resting unity.

Ricoeur explicitly addresses the specific problem of how we can understand ourselves as ethical agents, in which we make future-orientated decisions and seek to account for past actions. Narrative may still play an important role in establishing such agency. Narrative allows us to connect a sense of ourselves as motivated actors now, with both past influences and hopes for the future. The idea of a character within a story is useful for understanding motivated actions insofar as the idea of motivation is at once a projection into the future and what we want for ourselves, and an appeal to who we are now, often in the context of how our history has shaped us. Visual art however is capable of working with narrative. Thus, if we want to maintain an account of ethical agency as part of our account of self, then narrative can be integrated into a broader, corporeal understanding of the hermeneutics of the self. This is clear in Bourgeois's tableaux pieces: *Oedipus* (2003) and *The Reticent Child* (2003). Small figures, depicting different stages of life, tell a story, though not in a simple linear form. The former plays out the myth of Oedipus, the latter of Bourgeois's relationship to her son, Alain, as he grows from child to man. But narrative is only part of the significance of these works. Equally, it is only part of the process of self-construction. We need a hermeneutics of the self which combines narrative meaning as one strand of interpretation operating simultaneously with other interpretative activities to form who we are. Narrative can support the interpretation of a motivated actor, but the self is not reducible to character in this sense.

Julia Kristeva argues that 'Bourgeois' work juxtaposes without breakage and connects without isolation' (Kristeva 2007: 250). I think that what Kristeva has perceived is that Bourgeois offers us an example of what Ricoeur sought in plot: a concordant discordance. Unlike plot, however, her visual art can show how this concordance is between, sometimes discordant, simultaneous processes. Emplotment was a solution to the problem of unity across time. Visual art shows us how diverse, simultaneous processes can create form concurrently and interactively. We have seen that Bourgeois's work can capture ambivalence and unite heterogenous interpretations. A model of the hermeneutics of the self which learns from visual art is one in which interpretations create form through their interactions; the tensions, alliances, incorporations which occur all contribute to a process of unification or form-giving. The forms that emerge weave together diverse and competing interpretations.

We cannot say in advance what level of unity is adequate to constitute a self or what this self will look like. One attraction of a narrative theory of the self is that we know what constitutes a plot and can specify minimum requirements for a plot, which allows us to specify minimum requirements of selfhood. However, while this appeals to defenders of narrative theories of the self it can also be seen as a limitation of this model of self-construction, on which we stipulate in advance what forms are possible. I am aiming at a model of self-construction which instead leaves room for experiment and for challenges to existing templates of selfhood. We will either be able to interpret a coherent form in an artwork or not. Similarly, we do not need to define exactly what is needed to be a self in order to recognise ourselves as one.

A theory of self-construction involves interpretation. But there are multiple and diverse processes of interpretation which a narrative theory of the self fails to capture. Multiple processes of construction are sometimes collaborating with, and supporting, each other, mixing and binding together, sometimes competing and pulling apart. To equate self-construction with emplotment both ignores ways in which we are continually being constructed and the extent to which our self-construction is not under the control of a single, stable and conscious agency. The idea of a single author is challenged both by the complexity of bodily processes and drives that operate to produce any given self and by the actions of other selves and groups of selves. Thus, emplotment both overlooks ways in which we are being shaped and restricts the ways in which we could shape ourselves.

My account of a corporeal hermeneutics of the self follows the circular pattern of Ricoeur's theory of emplotment. The possible forms of self that can emerge in processes of self-construction are shaped by artistic activities and our reception of them, and these artistic activities also draw on a field of agential activity which makes possible artistic interpretations and representations. For Ricoeur, narrative selves draw on the literary realisation of a character in a plot, but writers can only form plots from human action because human activity has a prenarrative form that is susceptible to emplotment. The corporeal hermeneutics I am proposing is also a hermeneutics in which the interpretative activities of the artist influence a cultural sphere in which the interpretative activities of self-construction operate, and at the same time the various activities of the hermeneutics of the self contribute to the context of meaningful forms and action which artists can represent and express. There is continuity and interaction between the form-giving processes of self-construction and the form-giving activity of art making. However, once we allow that a broader set of processes than emplotment contribute to self-construction, a broader set of artistic practices can be seen to be part of this circular process of enabling, and being enabled by, and influencing and being influenced by, selves and their activities. These include artistic practices which concern our corporeality. Thus, the forms of bodily realisation that are possible are shaped by existing representations of the body in painting, sculpture and dance, and the styles of comportment available to us in our society. Interpretations of bodily drives create but are also constrained by a cultural and artistic world. The cultural and the bodily thus have no clear demarcation. There is porosity between the construction of culture and the construction of the self, as well as circularity.

Given the interdependence of the social/cultural field and the hermeneutics of the self, I want to turn now to the problem introduced in Chapter 1 in my discussion of Foucault, of how a cultural and social sphere structured by power relations influences processes of self-construction and how various artworks have highlighted the operation of power and how it affects the development and expression of selves.

This critical function of artworks can create the space for experimentation, which can operate on both the level of self-construction and of social change, and which I will turn to in the final chapter.

NOTES

1. I use medium to refer to different types of art practice and artworks, such as painting or photography, rather than (as it is sometimes also used) to refer to the specific materials out of which a given artwork is made, such as stone, oil, watercolour, etc.

2. Nixon offers a detailed reading of Bourgeois's work in terms of a dialogue with Kleinian psychoanalytic theory, in which she suggests that Bourgeois's sculptures can be seen as part-objects (2005).

3. Bourgeois felt traumatised by her childhood realisation that her governess Sadie was having an affair with her charismatic father. This produced an intense sense of betrayal for herself and her mother as well as a complicated web of jealously and guilt. Bourgeois has said that her sculpture *Destruction of the Father* depicts the family dining table. She describes the sculpture as one in which the father has been 'dismembered' by his family (Kuspit 1988: 25). Bourgeois presents her own sculpture in Freudian terms: the children and long-suffering wife having ripped apart and begun to devour the dominant and tyrannical patriarch. It involves destruction through incorporation, allowing simultaneous revenge and unification with the ambivalent object of anger and desire and thus the expression of both murderous and sexual feelings towards the father. This particular narrative is part of Bourgeois's – who participated in years of analysis – own self-understanding. This sculpture, and the story attached to it, provide evidence of the need to express and integrate powerful drives regardless of whether we agree with the particular story concerning the drive aims, and alleged repression and return, in relation to Bourgeois's family history. That Bourgeois was deeply affected by her father's behaviour is clear. We can see the sculpture as an expression and working through of the drives as she describes them, or we might consider also the construction of a narrative around Sadie and the family dining table as part of the creative work Bourgeois undertakes, and see this interpretation as part of the work of maintaining the self. As I discussed in Chapter 1, a hermeneutic account is always faced with the problem that we cannot claim to have access to a 'truth' free from such interpretation.

4. *Refusing What We Are*

INTRODUCTION

Thus far, I have argued that there is no given self which is able to account for the complexity of our experience, rather the self is continually constructed, creating a unity between a multiplicity of processes. This construction involves active interpretations and incorporates a variety of interpretative practices. It is thus usefully characterised as a 'hermeneutics of the self'. I have argued further that emplotment as a model of self-construction is an oversimplification of the hermeneutics of the self. It neglects the multiplicity of simultaneous processes that can and do contribute to the continual production and maintenance of a self. Further, it neglects the corporeality of self-construction and in doing so it overlooks that these processes have their own material imperatives that evade the control of a central agent or author. The model of emplotment, therefore, oversimplifies the agency of self-construction. But the myth of a single author of self-construction is challenged by the, by turns, recalcitrance and effervescence of multiple bodily processes and, sometimes unconscious, drive activity, which refuse and escape a simple trajectory. This myth is also challenged by the effects of technologies of the self, discussed in Chapter 1, and understood to incorporate various social practices, cultural consumption, structuration of space and vision, rituals, etc., that, as Foucault maintains, operate on, or induce us to operate on, 'our bodies and souls, thoughts, conduct, and way of being, so as to transform' ourselves (Foucault 1988: 18), in accordance with the strategies of other selves and groups of selves. Visual art can itself operate as such a technology. We may employ technologies of the self deliberately according to our own goals, the potential for which I will return to in the next chapter, but they may also be employed in accordance with the goals of others and shape us in further unintended ways.

In this chapter, I want to return to Foucault's understanding of power, which can help us to elaborate the way the social and cultural world not only constrains self-construction but, through various technologies of the self, operates on self-construction in ways that reinforce power structures. This makes self-construction, and deconstruction and reconstruction, integral to the possibility of political and social change. If we are to resist the extent of control exerted on us, and the structures of dominance this sustains, then the range of these technologies – how they currently operate to create what Foucault calls a subjugated self and how they could be employed to create alternative forms of selfhood – needs to be explored. As I discussed in Chapter 1, the ways in which we are constructed are inherently prone to covering themselves over or disguising themselves. We need to recognise the diversity of technologies of the self, and how such technologies, including the production and consumption of visual art itself, operate on and through bodies. The aim of this chapter is to consider the role that visual art has to play in a critical exposure of how these technologies, including visual art itself, operate to produce a subjugated self or to limit the possibilities of self-construction. These processes include the creation of particular political and cultural identities, such as religion, gender and race, which are an important part of our individual identity or sense of ourselves as individuals, for instance forming part of the context in which we understand our feelings, projects and motivations to act. They also concern how we relate to these identities, whether for instance we feel constrained by them, or able to detach from them. The construction of, and attachment to, such political and cultural identities is not synonymous with self-construction but can be, and I would suggest in current society is, a significant part of it. Resisting subjugation then requires that the ties to our particular identity, and its incorporation of these culturally recognised identities, are loosened and the fixity of both our particular identity as an individual, and the cultural and social identities it connects with, are challenged. It requires that we can reshape or reject the identities society offers us. This requires the work of demonstrating the numerous ways in which selves, including the details and significance of the identities they incorporate, are constructed and the implication of these various modes of construction in regimes of power.

After recapping Foucault's understanding of power and further elaborating the role of the subject within it, I will discuss the example of gender. Gender identity is a potent example of both how being tied to a particular identity can be oppressive, and of the various ways which exceed narrative and language that are continually working to produce, and hold us to, a particular identity. Revealing the variety of ways in which identities such as genders are constructed is a crucial stage in resisting a form of subjectivity that ties us to these identities and maintains these identities in rigid forms. In this chapter, I will focus on the important role that visual artworks have to play in this critical work. In particular, I will discuss the art of Cindy Sherman. Sherman's work provides a critique of images of women and their role in the construction of identity, which includes the complicity of the audience, thus highlighting that the hermeneutics of the self is not a solitary or autonomous activity but one that is intersubjective and embedded in power relations. Despite the focus on image and surface, however, Sherman's later works assert the presence of a corporeality that cannot be subsumed by cultural tropes of femininity. Thus, we will see that emplotment is a constricted theory of self-construction both because it obscures various technologies that are already constructing us and because it is prescriptive about how we could be constructed and thus what kind of self we could be. The oversimplification of the hermeneutics of the self can itself operate to limit self-construction and thus reinforce existing forms of subjectivity and the power regimes they sustain. Just as the claim that the self is given can impose a normative template on who we can be, so can restrictive theories of how a self can be constructed. Visual image, however, will also turn out to be limiting of the possibilities of selfhood. The disruption achieved by critical artworks which address the role of images and of technologies that shape our bodies can create the space to experiment with what we are and test the limits of what a self can be, but we will also need technologies that seek to include what both plot and coded image work to exclude.

THE SUBJUGATED SELF

For Foucault, there is no self prior to or apart from the various processes of self-construction or hermeneutic activity that we engage in, such as the ancient practices of the 'care of the self' to which he turns his attention in his late lectures at the Collège de France (Foucault 2005), and the last two volumes of the *History of Sexuality* (Foucault 1985, 1986). As Timothy O'Leary puts it: 'What fascinates Foucault in Classical Greek thought is that there the practice of self-care, self-formation and auto-poesis appears not to be thought in terms of a pre-given self, or subject, which must be either deciphered or validated' (2002: 120). O'Leary suggests that Foucault is operating with an understanding of the self as 'the more or less homogenous coming together of our modes of subjectivity' (2002: 120). This 'subject is not a substance, it is a form which is constituted through practices, which are always specific to particular social and historical contexts' (O'Leary 2002: 111).

There are various technologies of the self which contribute to these modes of subjectivity and the forms of selfhood that can emerge from their interaction. In Chapter 1, I considered Foucault's example of the architectural prison design of the Panopticon, in which a prisoner never knows when they are observed, thereby creating an interiority through self-observation. This technology's most explicit instantiation can be found in Bentham's prison design, but it is present outside of prisons. CCTV, classroom layouts, records of all our online activity, these give us the constant sense of being monitored and encourage us to be a subject who therefore monitors themselves and conforms to social norms. I also discussed Foucault's account of the confessional practices extending beyond the Christian Pastoral and into various secular contexts such as the patient/doctor relationship. Other technologies of the self that Foucault discusses include the 'constant writing activity' of the Hellenistic age in which 'the experience of oneself was intensified and widened by virtue of this act of writing. A whole field of experience opened which earlier was absent' (Foucault 1988: 28). Another is the ancient practices of the interpretation of dreams (Foucault 1988: 39). In his historical analysis of changing technologies of the self, Foucault is interested in how different technologies of the self can operate to produce different ways of the self relating to the self. He contrasts ancient technologies of the self to the later total obedience of the monk which is 'a sacrifice of the self, of the subject's own will. This is a new technology of the self' (Foucault 1988: 45). As I will discuss further below, his claim is that contemporary technologies of the self take on this Christian Pastoral form and produce a subjugated subject, who is tied to their own identity in a constraining way.

The technologies or practices which constitute the self or subject are always, according to Foucault, operating in the context of power relations and framed and influenced by power strategies. As explained in Chapter 1, power according to Foucault is not a thing that one possesses but rather something that is exercised on and through the actions of subjects. 'Power exists only when it is put into action, even if, of course, it is integrated into a disparate field of possibilities brought to bear on permanent structures' (Foucault 1982: 788). He provides a useful summary of his understanding of the complexity and all-pervasiveness of power in the first volume of his *History of Sexuality* (1978: 94–6). It is important to note that power is not purely negative or repressive; power operates by getting us to do and say things, it is thus productive: including – as is pertinent to our discussion of forms of subjectivity – producing as well as confining ways of being a self. Power does not declare itself as power; it is itself a tactic of power to encourage a simplistic view of power as top-down oppression and keep its own complexity and subtlety disguised. In fact, power operates from multiple points and in all directions, though there may be advantages to particular groups sustained by a particular network of power relations, and rigidities in the relations and practices that form. Foucault argues that power is immanent to other relationships, and is both productive of relationships, such as social class, and an effect of them. Finally, Foucault claims that power can be intentional without being subjective. That is, it can be understood in terms of the tactics which serve various aims and objectives, such as influencing the birth rate of a population, without needing to be the conscious choice of particular individuals.

Is Foucault's claim – that the kind of self we are is shaped by a complex network of power relations – a convincing one? I argued in Chapter 1 that the self is best understood as formed from the interpretations of various bodily processes and practices. If we view the self as constructed through and incorporating multiple processes, along with Freud, Nietzsche and Foucault, this allows us to better account for the mutability and complexity of our experiences. It is not difficult to find examples of social and cultural practices that contribute to this construction; looking beyond the examples that Foucault collects from Ancient Greece, to the Christian Pastoral, asylums, prisons and educational establishments, we are now faced with a plethora of examples of self-fashioning, such as detox diets, Facebook status updates, posting Instagram pictures and mindfulness. Another example is the division of space, for example into public and private. Griselda Pollock details how this territorial mapping 'structured the very meaning of the terms masculine and feminine with its mythic boundaries' and 'regulated women's and men's behaviour' (Pollock 1988: 69). The idea of narrating our lives, or telling various stories about ourselves and our actions, can also be understood as one among many technologies of the self. It is also not difficult to see how the various ways in which these practices develop modes of subjectivity can serve other purposes at the same time, from selling face creams to maintaining political regimes. The modes of subjectivity that are produced by these practices may be integral to these aims, or a by-product of them. Foucault is not suggesting a conspiracy theory in which we see such operations of power as an intentional plot. His suggestion is that we view the habits, practices, representations, etc., that contribute to a hermeneutics of the self in terms of power tactics, in the sense that various aims may be furthered by their uptake. This framework of analysis allows us to understand how such technologies can gather momentum and become entrenched.

For Foucault, then, various practices that shape us are operations of power, and the formation of a particular kind of subject can itself be a tactic of power – producing a disciplined subject that conforms to certain behaviours. The kind of subjects we are now, formed in the context of a particular system of power, are according to Foucault subjugated subjects, in contrast to the comparative autonomy of the ancient selves who cared for the self with the aim of self-improvement and self-mastery. The modern state is faced with the challenge of combining individualisation and totalisation (Foucault 1982: 782). That is, it must both monitor and control individuals in their specificity and control whole populations in all aspects of their behaviour. To this end, it has adapted the pastoral power of Christianity, which looked after both the flock as a whole and the soul and salvation of each individual member. As such it is linked with the production of truth about the subject themselves, as demonstrated in the activity of confession (Foucault 1982: 783). In the Christian Pastoral, our desires and thoughts were integral to our salvation and thus it was the business of the priest to induce us to reveal them. In a modern context, well-being and health in this life replace the soul's salvation in the next, and the mechanisms and operatives that concern themselves with the intimate habits of the populace multiply, encompassing doctors, educators, police and family. Hence, the modern subject experiences excessive, continual and all-encompassing control, for example in the way medical professionals have control over our bodies, life and death (Foucault 1982: 780). Therefore, many social movements and activist struggles are engaged in asserting both an individual's right to be different and also working against that which 'ties him to his own identity in a constraining way' (Foucault 1982: 781). This emphasises for Foucault how we face a:

> form of power [which] applies itself to immediate everyday life which categorizes the individual, marks him by his own individuality, attaches him to his own identity, imposes a law of truth on him which he must recognize and which others must recognize in him. It is a form of power which makes individuals subjects. There are two meanings of the word 'subject': subject to someone else by control and dependence; and tied to his own identity by a conscience or self-knowledge. Both meanings suggest a form of power which subjugates and makes subject to. (Foucault 1982: 781)

Given that what we are as subjects and who we are in terms of the identities we lay claim to are both emmeshed in the context of power relations, resisting particular power strategies, and more radical disruption of ossified power hierarchies, requires changing the kinds of subject we are:

> Maybe the target nowadays is not to discover what we are but to refuse what we are. We have to imagine and to build up what we could be to get rid of this kind of political 'double bind,' which is this simultaneous individualization and totalization of modern power structures.
>
> The conclusion would be that the political, ethical, social, philosophical problem of our days is not to try to liberate the individual from the state and from the state's institutions but to liberate us both from the state and from the type of individualization which is linked to the state. We have to promote new forms of subjectivity through the refusal of this kind of individuality which has been imposed on us for several centuries. (Foucault 1982: 785)

Foucault thus places refusing a particular kind of individuality at the heart of resistance to social and political dominance and as necessary to escaping an all-pervading control over our subjectivity. To this end he suggests the need to promote new forms of subjectivity. Given that the form of subjectivity that Foucault suggests we need to refuse involves us being tied to our identity, this suggests that the new forms of subjectivity we need to promote will involve both a refusal of existing identities and of identity as something fixed or determining of us. This will involve an awareness of how these identities are not revealed as the truth of what we always are, as claimed in the confessional model, but rather constructed in the context of power relations.

Crucially, the pervasiveness of power relations does not mean that they cannot be resisted. Even while our actions are reactions to power strategies, they are not fully determined by the strategies they react against (Foucault 1982: 791–2). Foucault insists that: 'Power is exercised only over free subjects, and only insofar as they are free. By this we mean individual or collective subjects who are faced with a field of possibilities in which several ways of behaving, several reactions and diverse comportments, may be realized' (Foucault 1982: 790). While 'power is always present', it is also the case that:

> these power relations are [. . .] mobile, reversible and unstable. It should also be noted that power relations are possible only insofar as these subjects are free. If one of them were completely at the other's disposal and became his thing, an object on which he could wreak boundless and limitless violence, there wouldn't be any relations of power. Thus, in order for power relations to come into play, there must be at least a certain degree of freedom on both sides [. . .] This means that in power relations there is necessarily the possibility of resistance. (Foucault 1997: 192)

In Foucault's account, therefore, there is the possibility of acting differently and thus the possibility of taking up new technologies and counter-technologies of the self. The subject we are now is formed in the context of power relations, but it is not fixed. What and who we are is open to revision. Indeed, historically we can see the continuous creation of new subjectivities: 'in the course of their history men have never stopped constructing themselves, that is to say continually displacing their subjectivity, constituting themselves in an infinite and multiple series of different subjectivities' (Foucault 1994: 75). This process of revision – when accompanied by analysis of power relations and an understanding of how they can operate through technologies of the self to influence self-construction – can be directed in a way that breaks free from the modes allowed by, and supportive of, the current patterns of dominance.[1]

THE SUBJUGATED WOMAN

I want now to consider a concrete example of how various technologies of the self can shape our identity and tie us to that identity in an oppressive way. Gender, the idea that our sexual differences translate to a mode of subjectivity involving a complex set of ways of appearing, moving, behaving, valuing and expressing ourselves, and relating to others that can be characterised as more or less female or male, provides a potent example of how culture shapes the kind of subjects we become. The various ways we represent men and women, ranging from literature to TV adverts, the various established practices we engage in, such as team sports and grooming, the examples of how bodies should hold or comport themselves, how they should be used, the demarcation of space that we are permitted in, all influence and constrain variously gendered subjects. The cultural source material that we draw on in our hermeneutics of the subject, and social expectations of what it is to be a male or female subject, and that we should be one or the other, can encompass various subdivisions or types, such as the effete man and the femme fatale, but these representations still influence how we identify ourselves, and how we behave because of our identity, in potentially constraining ways.

Feminist analysis explicitly connects the ways in which women are expected to not only dress, groom and comport themselves but understand and value themselves – that is the ways in which they are tied to the identity (or a subset of approved identities) of woman (or a feminine type such as girl, mother, hag, etc.) – with the maintenance of a social and political order which disadvantages and oppresses them. One example that Meyers gives in her *Gender in the Mirror*, is the effective marginalisation from the public sphere, and psychological cost of this, for older women (2002: 148–66). Another is how expectations around motherhood put pressure on women to be a certain kind of mother, and the failure to live up to this again carries a psychological cost and devalues childless women (Meyers 2002: 30–57). The exclusion of ambiguity around motherhood, and the costs incurred by the expectations that women be mothers, and be delighted to be mothers, is something we explored already with the work of Louise Bourgeois, who experienced the tensions of trying to be an artist and a mother. The complex emotions around motherhood that Bourgeois's work expresses are so forceful because they have been mostly repressed and denied in portrayals of motherhood. A third theme that Meyers analyses is the portrayal of women as vain and concerned with appearance (2002: 99–147). Women are encouraged to spend a huge amount of time and money on their looks to fulfil a notion of what it is to be a woman successfully. While capitalism's tentacles reach into the male market too, the scale of marketing around beauty does not yet approach that aimed at women. This concern with looking good, in a highly prescriptive way, involves resources that could be spent elsewhere, a trivialisation and designation as superficial that undermines efforts to be taken seriously and have one's interests represented and heard in work and politics, and sets one up for unhappiness if one fails to meet the standard of beauty – which given the impossible standards presented by the industries that make money from the quest for ever greater perfection is felt by almost all women. Even for those who meet the socially set beauty standard, with its racial and age biases, there is the double bind of being blamed for vanity and frippery (Meyers 2002: 146). These are just some of the ways in which living up to the image of woman bears a cost.

Of course, there is no single definition of femininity. Meyers astutely recognises that a variety of acceptable options is crucial to the maintenance of gender stereotypes that prop up our current system of power relations. There are enough ways of being a women or a man to allow adaptation of the tropes to particular situations and needs and ensure that men are able to hold on to misogynist and sexist views that advantage them and 'have enough latitude to craft a form of sexism that is responsive to their personal needs and life circumstances' (Meyers 2002: 187). This adaptability and variety also appeals to how women may become complicit in sustaining gender tropes, having been accorded some room to feel they control what kind of women they are when they select from the library of acceptable feminine types.

Clearly visual representation and images are a crucial part of this cultural stock of possible identities, and thus of establishing our self-understanding as men and women (or as fitting neither category) and shaping our hermeneutics of the self as gendered selves. That representations, including those created in visual art, do not merely reflect but rather work to shape the kind of gendered subjects we are is well documented by Elizabeth Cowie, Diana Tietjens Meyers and Griselda Pollock (Cowie 2000; Meyers 2002; Pollock 1988), among others. Pollock, for instance, observes that '[p]ictures, photographs, films, etc., are addressed to us as their viewers and work upon us by means of winning our identification with those versions of masculinity and femininity which are represented to us' (Pollock 1988: 34).

The effects of visual representation on women's self-construction reach back into the history of painting, accelerating with the advent of photography and the growth of advertising. Examples of visual art's role in enforcing gender identity include the woman-with-mirror motif. John Berger highlighted the function of mirrors in depictions of women, suggesting that they were used frequently as a symbol of women's vanity, but more than this they functioned 'to make the woman connive in treating herself as, first and foremost, a sight' (Berger 1972: 51). Meyers documents the use of mirrors specifically in relation to the myth and concept of narcissism. This motif, she says, occurs frequently in the history of art. Men are rarely seen with mirrors; if they are, it is the context of the painter doing a self-portrait, to emphasise the value of prudence, or it is used to portray them as effeminate. Women, however, are often painted contemplating their beauty or engaged in their toilette and 'paintings depicting the vice of vanity are perceived as archetypal images of femininity' (Meyers 2002: 107). Meyers cites the examples of paintings of Venus by Titian, Velázquez and Rubens, among others. Pollock's earlier work offers another example of the mirror motif in her discussion of Dante Gabriel Rossetti's paintings of the ideal of the beautiful woman. In Rossetti's work and the cultural moment he crystallises, Pollock traces the formation of a visual representation now prevalent in advertising, which 'naturalized woman as image, beautiful to look at, defined by her "looks"' (1988: 121). Pollock suggests that these paintings offer a 'fantasy of visual perfection' which conflate a beautiful picture with 'woman as beautiful' (1988: 122). The pictures combine '*physical* loveliness' of the woman portrayed, always a type associated with one of Rosetti's models and never a portrait of a model in her specificity, with a 'remote *look*' (1988: 126). Rosetti's paintings, Pollock argues, 'organize visual pleasure' (1988: 128), such that woman is seen and pursued, but never sees, and remains remote (1988: 153).

Foucault understood that the discourses that influence us, which include visual images, include silence and thus encompass what is not represented or made visible (Foucault 1978: 27). Equally important to how images are used is a lack of images or what is not portrayed in our society. The ways in which we are able to appear are limited. This absence can indicate other social constraints at play. For instance, Frances Borzello gives a detailed account of the evolution of women's self-portraiture (2016). Women artists were faced with barriers to being recognised as professionals and earning a living as artists. To succeed they needed to be seen as attractive but also as respectable and free from scandal. They thus eschewed workwear in their self-presentation, and there is therefore an absence of paintings of women in the act of painting. It was not until the nineteenth century, Borzello argues, that the 'necessity for ingratiating femininity' began to recede and allow for greater self-expression and more confident professional self-assertation (2016: 131). This kind of art history analysis offers artworks as evidence of the limits on how women could constitute themselves as subjects, but also testifies to art's role in reinforcing, even if at other times also subverting, these limits on subjectivity.

What is shown (and not shown) in paintings reveals the presence of other technologies at work, such as the demarcation of spaces women are permitted to occupy, or roles they are permitted to take, as emphasised in Borzello's discussion. But it also limits the cultural resources we can draw on in expressing ourselves and constituting our identities. The prevalence of stereotypes and the lack of positive images with which to identify work to limit the ways in which people are able to interpret themselves, and thus the identities they can take up and develop, and how constraining, or conversely fluid, these identities are in their operation. This in turn ties us in an oppressive way to the identities that society allows us. Sonia Boyce is an artist who explores the difficulty of expressing herself as a black woman within the context of entrenched cultural racism. Her *From Tarzan to Rambo: English Born 'Native' Considers her Relationship to the Constructed/Self Image and her Roots in Reconstruction* (1987) consists of repeated photo-booth pictures of herself which reference both the cartoon images that border the piece and media images of blackness in general, including the trope of the voodoo trance. The work points to the power of stereotypes but also to the absence of alternative images and the lack of space in which to develop them. This work shows us that the stereotypes go beyond the stories that are told about people, and thus the narratives they are able to tell about themselves. The stereotypical expectations placed on people, to interpret themselves in ways that conform to expectations, encompass how we appear and how we inhabit and move our bodies, extending even to facial expressions (as in Boyce's work) and gestures.

Artworks that employ visual images and employ the body are thus part of the hermeneutics of the self and can be seen to have been part of tying us to our identities and reinforcing oppression. As technologies of the self they do not merely reflect but are complicit in producing particular identities and modes of being a self, by producing images, excluding and selecting, and structuring vision. What role, then, can visual artworks play in refusing rather than reinforcing oppressive identities?

HOW CAN WE REFUSE WHAT WE ARE?

According to Foucault our subjectivity is formed in the context of power relations, yet we can never step out of these power relations. So, our subjectivity will always be influenced by the power tactics of others, and the resources we draw on in constructing ourselves will be implicated in the network of power relations we inevitably operate within. If we are to change our subjectivity in ways that resist the objectives of others, and free ourselves from being chained to particular identities, we must cultivate an awareness of the complexity of how power operates. We can then hope to act in ways that subvert or resit these tactics, and not simply to serve as pawns in the maintenance of a disciplinary society. To refuse *what* we are in Foucault's sense will be to refuse to be fixed once and for all to any one identity, to escape the trap of identity, such as that which holds Bourgeois's *Femme Maison* in the role of housewife. But first we must refuse *who* we are, and untie ourselves from our current identities, to allow for new identities to be explored.

To change who we are, detaching from or altering our current identity, will require drawing on our existing cultural resources. In relation to the technologies of the self which we can employ to actively constitute ourselves, Foucault says in an interview: 'they are not something invented by the individual himself. They are models that he finds in his culture and are proposed, suggested, imposed, upon him by his culture, his society, his social group' (Foucault 1997: 191). We must, therefore, take up any such technologies in a self-aware way that recognises the various ends they may serve and allows us to challenge and subvert these aims. We can then hope to employ these technologies in ways that create new, alternative models of subjectivity, and thus by refusing various demarcated answers to who we are, we are able to refuse what we are – i.e. a subjugated subject with a rigid identity. To do so will require an understanding of the operation of power and continuous critical awareness of its presence.

This critical analysis can be extended beyond the specific case of gender to include figurations of race, age and sexuality, all of which influence how we interpret and present ourselves, and thus the selves that we construct. Once we recognise that the hermeneutics of the self is far broader than narrative, and that there are various modes of interpretation that shape us, sometimes in oppressive ways, then we recognise that taking control of our practices of self-construction cannot be limited to telling new stories about ourselves. If visual art has been complicit in the operation of power by perpetuating images of what it is to be a woman or a man, to be black, white, straight, gay, etc., in ways that constrain subjectivity, then visual art must engage in its own self-critique.

It is important that the critique of the visual image is not limited to theory. The power of the visual image over us depends on its visual form, influencing us in ways that we cannot undo at a purely conceptual level. It involves not a static image but a relationship between a viewer and the object viewed. Pollock suggests that feminists recognise that 'the very strucutres of viewing and taking pleasure in looking at images are implicated in oppressive regimes' (1988: 198). Exposing the role of visual images, and ways of looking at these images, through visual means allows a full understanding of its operation that cannot be reduced to words. It can also start to undo the insidious hold such images have on us at an affective level.

Visual artworks can thus effectively draw to our attention the power of the visual image in constraining our subjectivity and offer a critique that can destabilise this regime. This helps create the space to refuse who we are allowed to be within our current system of power relations. Before moving on in the next chapter to consider what explorations and experiments are possible once this space opens up, I want to consider the work of Cindy Sherman as an example of how visual artwork can perform this critical and destabilising function. This critical capacity of art to identify modes of self-construction has been analysed before, but it is worth returning to it in the context of my project before I turn to the positive potential of art as a technology of the self in forging alternative forms of subjectivity. This is worthwhile firstly because this critical phase is required to create the space for the creation of alternatives and to ensure that such alternatives are not simply co-opted in support of the existing modes of power, once again tying us to our own identities. Thus, the success of the critical work that artists have undertaken, and art historians and critics have recognised, is a precondition to the experimentation which I will focus on in my final chapter. But, secondly, the discussion of the critical function of art in highlighting the role of images will also reveal how image, like narrative, can operate as a prescriptive and limiting framework for selfhood. It will, therefore, highlight the importance of creative responses that go beyond those Meyers advocates, of re-appropriating images and forging counter-images (2002: 57).

Sherman is important because she does far more than catalogue media images and portrayals of femininity, she connects these images to the problem of how identity is established, and, crucially, she confronts us with our complicity as a viewer and consumer of images in this construction. However, her later work also reminds us of what is excess to image as well as to plot. Thus, this discussion serves the dual function of offering an example of how visual art, in contributing to the construction of identities through the use of image, serves as a technology of the self that is not reducible to narrative and can be complicit with power regimes, and of showing that the equation of self to image is prescriptive not just in terms of the particular images society permits but also in limiting selfhood to what images can contain.

CINDY SHERMAN: IMAGE AND IDENTITY

Cindy Sherman's work can be considered as both performance and photography. All her work takes the final form of still photography, with the exception of short films made at art school. In almost all her work she is her own model. The *Sex Pictures* (1992–6) and *Surrealist Pictures* (1993–4) which use dolls and mannequins are the main exceptions. In her photographs – from the *Untitled Film Stills* (1977–80), and numerous series of individually untitled works including her *Rear Screen Projections* (1980), wide format *Centrefolds* (1981), *Fairy Tales* (1985), *History Portraits* (1988–90) which recreate various historical masters, *Clowns* (2003–5) and more recently *Society Portraits* (2008) and ageing *Flappers* (2016–18) – she employs make-up, wigs, costumes, masks and later prosthetics to transform her appearance and present various characters. These props – in combination with background (in recent work using digital technology), lighting and photographic style – contribute to the production of multiple characters. Her characters have ranged from various cinematic feminine tropes to monstrous fairy tale creatures and eerie clowns.

In some of Sherman's works parody operates as a form of critique. This is arguably the case in her 'ugly' fashion images, commissioned by fashion houses and magazines once Sherman was an established artist, and showing women in designer clothes who might be described as despondent, inane, tense, etc. We can also read her ageing society women from the *Society Portraits*, heavily made up and surrounded by opulence and status symbols, and the desperate actors in the *Headshots* (2000) series, as parodies of attempts to hold on to youth. In both these series it is clear that the obvious, heavy make-up cannot help these women, whose careers as actors or rich housewives has traded on looks, to stay young and beautiful. In these pictures, with their obvious artifice, there is thus a pathos of lost youth and an accompanying loss of status and identity, combined with pathetic attempts to cling to it. Parody is most apparent in Sherman's early *Cover Girls* (1976). These five works take covers from women's magazines (*Cosmopolitan*, *Vogue*, *Family Circle*, *Redbook* and *Mademoiselle*). Three images are presented for each cover: one the original model, one of Sherman closely mimicking the cover girl's make-up and expression, and finally one that is pulling a strange face, mocking the original image. The desacralising effect of parody helps loosen the dominance of cultural imagery and destabilise the system it is intermeshed with. But more is needed.

Sherman's analysis of appearance, and the image, and its connection to identity in general and women's identity in particular, does far more than merely parody mass media. The multiple characters of her film stills point to the instability of identity. The way she is able to morph in and out of roles – with the use of both the costumes, make-up and wigs that disguise her presence as model and the background and photographic styles that code her within certain film genres – suggests that identity is mutable. They can thereby facilitate in cultivating a more fluid relationship to identity. In one image she is a 1950s' pin-up, in another the girl next door, in another the stoic working-class woman. In *Untitled Film Still #13* (1978), by donning a Bardot-style scarf, reaching up to a bookshelf above her in a way that emphasises her (very 1960s) rather pointed bust, she is the intellectual but sexy heroine of a *nouvelle vague* film. In *Untitled Film Still #54* (1980, Figure 4.1), wearing a short blonde wig and smart suit, she walks down a dark street, pulling up the collar of her coat in apprehension and thus evokes memories of the vulnerability of a Hitchcock blonde.

But this emphasis on artifice reduces these characters to their appearances. What does this tell us about the cultural construction of women's subjectivity? Sherman's work exposes the tendency to reduce women to the types that they might play in literature, film or advertising. Judith Williamson suggests that when we look at Sherman's work we see the women pictured *as* the stereotypical character, the trope, that is portrayed. If a woman's way of dressing, moving, generally presenting themselves is read as a code that defines them in terms of a cultural trope of femininity, then this narrow library of feminine types is limiting the modes of subjectivity available to them (Williamson 2006).

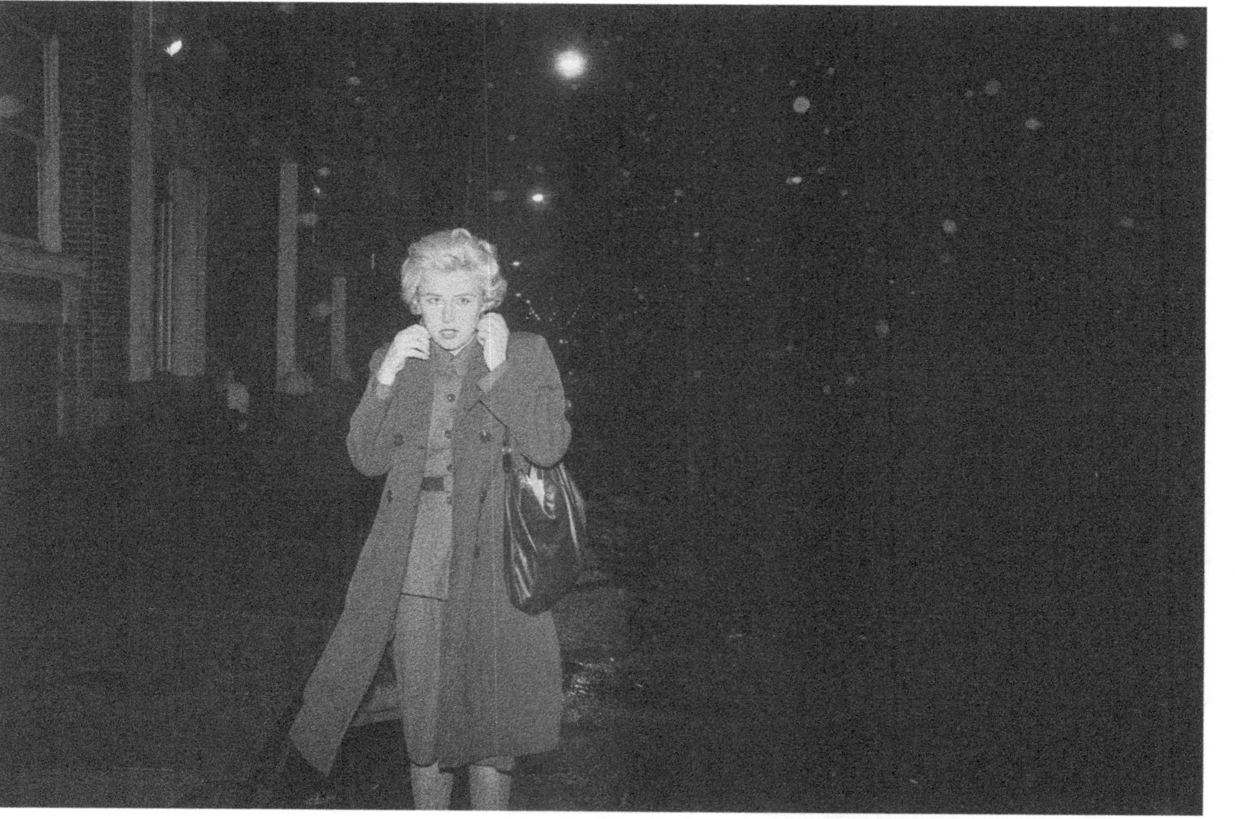

4.1 Cindy Sherman, *Untitled Film Still #54*, 1980, gelatin silver print, 20.3 × 25.4 cm. Courtesy of the artist and Metro Pictures New York

While the film stills present the possibility of taking on different types through dress and performance, these finite types offer us a very limited selection that constrains how a woman can interpret herself as a self, as does the requirement to be a 'type' at all.

The style of photography and the references to particular film genres that the photograph itself makes are crucial to this reduction of the women in Sherman's pictures to culturally specified types. Williamson illustrates this with specific examples: 'The low angle, crisp focus, and sharp contrasts of *Untitled Film Still #16* are part of the woman's sophisticated yet fragile image, just as the slightly soft focus and low contrast of *#40* are part of *her* more pastoral, Renoir-esque femininity' (2006: 40). Norman Bryson also emphasises the importance of the actual photograph, and not just what is in front of the camera when the picture is taken:

> Alter the lighting, focus, or grain of the print, and there are immediate consequences in the sense of 'identity' being fabricated. Sherman exposes the material underpinnings of identity-production, not only the theatrical codes of costume and gesture, but the photographic codes that come to join them. If graininess in the print makes the figure seem different (distanced or mysterious or disfigured), that proves beyond a doubt that what we had taken to be the source of the presence to which we respond – the figure, the referent, with its/her inwardness and depth – actually emanates from the materiality of the signifying work, from the photographic paper and the way it has been processed, from the apparatus of representation itself. (2006: 85)

The implication of designating various different characters in Sherman's series of *Untitled Film Stills*, on the basis of how she appears in a particular, stylised photograph is 'the elision of image and identity' (Williamson 2006: 39):

> In the 'Untiled Film Stills' we are constantly forced to recognize a visual style (often you could name the director) simultaneously with a type of femininity. The two cannot be pulled apart. The image suggests that there is a particular kind of femininity in the *woman* we see, whereas in fact the femininity is in the image itself, it *is* the image. (Williamson 2006: 40)

Women are not only limited to particular, acceptable cultural tropes of femininity, they are reduced to their appearance, to the projection of their image within a cultural field laden with signification.

Crucially, Williamson emphasises that we are the ones who in looking at Sherman's film pictures make the women into these character types. What Sherman's work shows us is how identity is not constructed autonomously but in relation to others that view us and in the context of a coded cultural and social field. Many of Sherman's works suggest the presence of a hidden voyeur. Part of the construction of her character's vulnerability is often the sense that she is being watched. In *Untitled Film Still #83* (1980), we experience the viewpoint of someone spying on the brunette in the trench coat with a camera. But the sense that there is someone watching some of the women in her stills is itself part of the coding of the women's role and her designation as a character type. It is not just a question of allowing us to experience the role of the voyeur or male gaze, rather Sherman shows us our active role in categorising the various heroines, and in so doing reducing them to the image – which is constructed both through the make-up and costume and the photographic style – that codes them. Sherman 'leads the viewer to *construct*' the identity of the woman based on the image of the women (Williamson 2006: 39), and thus the 'viewer is forced into complicity with the way these "women" are constructed' (Williamson 2006: 40).

The understanding that we gain from Sherman's images concerning how modes of female subjectivity are constructed can be used to free ourselves from their grip. But more than just allowing us to recognise the cultural codification involved, they allow us to be aware of our own participation in these processes of interpretation as consumers of culture. In keeping with Foucault's idea of technologies of the self, Meyers suggests that critique is a skill we need to develop and master through practice. For example,

> skills in interpreting and critiquing prevalent figurations of motherhood and skills in accessing and adapting figurative materials from diverse sources are necessary if women are to extricate themselves from matrigyno-idolatry and gain self-determination in respect to motherhood. (Meyers 2002: 55)

Experiencing our own involvement in interpreting Sherman's figure in her pictures as an 'abandoned lover', '1950s' career girl making her way in the big city', 'sophisticated seductress', etc., gives us a greater awareness of the ways in which cultural codes shape our interpretations, and a greater sensitivity to reductive tendencies to equate who someone is with their culturally mediated appearance, and to make this *what* they are as a fixed identity.

Of course, by evoking cinema the film stills evoke possible narratives. So, they could be held to support a narrative account of the construction of identity, even if at the same time they emphasise the importance of the material photograph and visual appearance to narrative interpretation. But if Sherman's images connect narrative to the construction of identity, they do so in a way that shows this process of cultural construction of selves as limiting and problematic. In many of the film stills, the character is incomplete unless we posit the content of a letter, a phone call or presence outside the shot. Williamson argues that in every still, 'the woman suggests something other than herself, she is never complete: a narrative has to be invoked' (Williamson 2006: 43). The weeping women with half-packed suitcase in *Untitled Film Still #12* (1978) is running away from something or someone, someone has made her desperate, forced her to leave. But in this narrative the woman is defined by the actions of others, 'it is this imprintedness itself which seems to constitute femininity' (Williamson 2006: 43). If the dominant narrative of femininity is restrictive, and inherently passive, then women need alternative forms of interpretation with which to construct alternative identities that enable them to refuse who they are according to an oppressive culture.

WHEN THE IMAGE BUCKLES

Despite the focus on appearance and construction, the body, as something that cannot be reduced to cultural codification, arguably still asserts itself in Sherman's work. Sherman's *Centrefolds* reference soft porn, taking the wide format of a double-page magazine spread. They offer us various women in private and vulnerable moments. The view from above suggests to many a predatory gaze and has often been read as a critique of the pornographic mode of viewing women. Even at this level they reveal the presence of drives in the form of sexual desire. Krauss, however, suggests that in these images there is something else – an 'animality, the body clenched in a kind of subhuman fixation' (Krauss 2006: 118). If Krauss is right that there is a sense of animality in the *Centrefolds*, which we might understand as a corporeality that cannot be reduced to a culturally recognisable human identity, then I think this is more overt in the subsequent *Fairy Tales*. In *Untitled #140* (1985), Sherman portrays a recumbent, female figure in the undergrowth, her face part human, part pig, her hands gently touching her snout. The highly sinister *Untitled #156* (1985, Figure 4.2) is a kneeling figure sifting through the pebbles and shells of the shoreline, her blackened teeth are highlighted, their sharpness suggests the possibility of rendering raw flesh. We move beyond the human and evoke the animal, and the monstrous. By the *Disasters* series we are left with bloodstains, dismembered body parts, flesh, bone, decay. *Untitled #236* (1987) depicts what seems to be cartilage, blood, mould. *Untitled #235* (1987) is similar but suggests the hallucinatory hints of human features. In place of a neatly constructed character we have the processes of flesh, and its decay.

Bryson, like Krauss, argues that Sherman's late work indicates the presence of precisely that which cannot be reduced to the codes through

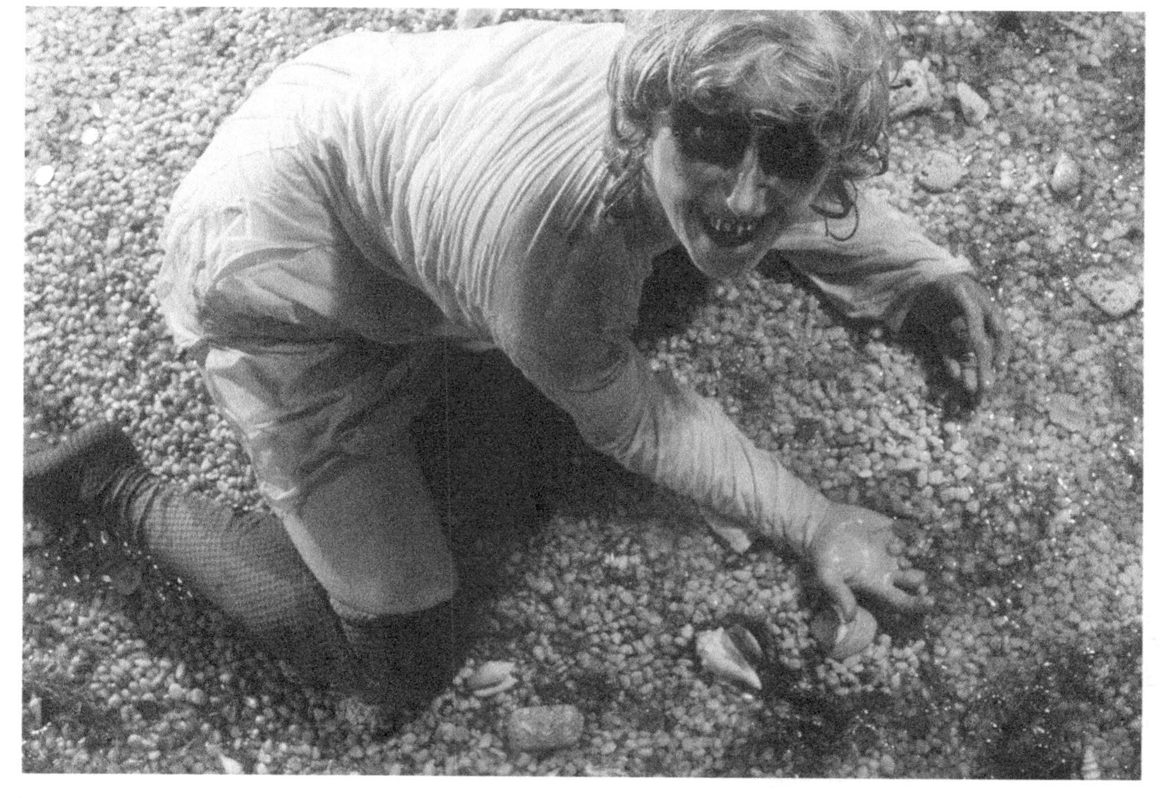

4.2 Cindy Sherman, *Untitled #156*, 1985, chromogenic colour print 123.2 × 181.6 cm. Courtesy of the artist and Metro Pictures New York

which her various characters are constructed, namely the body. While in her early work the body 'has been worked by the codes and conventions of representation to a point of saturation' (Bryson 2006: 85), we see in later series such as the *Fairy Tales* the 'body as that which cannot, will not, be sublimated into signifying space' (Bryson 2006: 87). Despite its evocation of stories the *Fairy Tales* series of pictures offers a body that cannot be captured by narrative interpretation: 'Language can only point towards this aspect of the body, cannot grasp its fleshiness and dampness, its excess beyond signification' (Bryson 2006: 89). But an entirely coded, readable visual image is also inadequate to the task. Bryson offers a powerful reading of Sherman's post-1985 work when he writes:

> Like language, visual representation can only find analogies and comparisons for this body [. . .] At the edges of representation or behind it hovers a body you will know about only because these inadequate stand-ins, which are there simply to mark a limit or boundary to representation, are able to conjure up a penumbra of something lying beyond representability. The penumbra indicates that discourse-as-sight cannot quite detect this region or bring it into focus. Yet insofar as the spectator has the sense that sight is not able comfortably to scan the penumbra (the gaze bouncing off the from the image, like an arrow hitting a shield), a certain nausea arises that unmistakably announces the advent of the real. Not because the image shows this or that horrible thing [. . .] the horror is never *in* the representation, but around it. (Bryson 2006: 89)

Bryson argues that in the face of this depiction of the bodily, rather than the figure of the body, the image buckles. What the horror, the affect within us as viewers, suggests to us is a body beyond codification, beyond discourse, beyond the disciplinary conditioning chronicled by Foucault. It is the 'the disciplinary's stumbling block' (2006: 91). In these pictures we find a 'monstrosity [which] is that of all the amorphous secretions that fall back into the subject as rejects from the disciplinary arena' (Bryson 2006: 92). The horror that lurks beyond the image, the flesh and excretions that invade some, are the 'mass of residues created as waste products from the theater of the cultural imaginary, where the subject assumes and internalizes its repertories of sanctioned and conventional appearances' (Bryson 2006: 92).

Given that Sherman has shown us how female identity and image are elided, if as Bryson aptly observes the image in her late work 'buckles' then so does identity. These waste products, the bodily forces and processes that cannot be captured in the processes of codification that Sherman's early work so artfully illustrated, are a menace to the culturally sanctified subject's stability. After her beautiful, witty, film stills come works that show us what does not fit the mould, what cannot be pressed into a plot, or a cinematic type, or a pictorial archetype. We return to the material processes that we observed in Louise Bourgeois's work, processes which evade static capture.

CONCLUSION

Critical works by visual artists can illustrate how representations of the body and constructions of coded images can be employed to shape subjectivity in potentially constraining and oppressive ways. By bringing these processes to our attention three important steps are taken. Firstly, in exposing processes of self-construction we recognise the self as a product of construction (as opposed to something given). Hence, the idea of stable identity, and the equation of the self with this identity, is undermined, such that the possibility of changing who and what we are presents itself. The ties that bind us to our identity are thus loosened and the rigidity of any particular identity is questioned. We can reshape identities and move between identities. Secondly, in showing the power operations involved in, and the possibly oppressive effects of, the construction of our identity, we are motivated to change our identity and our relationship to it. Finally, in showing us our own engagement in processes of interpretation that work to tie people to their identities, we develop the skills and awareness to take up the challenge of changing who and what we are with a sensitivity to the operation of technologies of the self. An awareness of how technologies of the self serve various power aims is necessary if we are not to simply recreate ourselves in ways that remain subjugated. But in recognising the potential of these technologies we can also furnish ourselves with resources to employ in the (continual) construction (and reconstruction) of a more autonomous subject. Crucially, visual art can draw our attention to the operation of technologies that are overlooked in narrative accounts of self-construction. In our discussion of Sherman's work, we saw one example of how visual artworks can illustrate and draw to our attention various processes of codification that influence our self-construction. Her work demonstrates the significance of visual images in this process. But it also demonstrates the complicity of the viewer in equating image and identity. Visual art can thus illustrate that the role of the viewer, and the particular gaze they take up, are also subject to construction. We are always being constructed in a variety of ways that cannot be reduced to emplotment, and refusing particular identities and being tied to our identities requires our awareness of these various technologies of the self, including the visual technologies at play in film, advertising and the art world.

But with Sherman's later work we were also reminded of corporeality that is not reducible to these codes, and the presence of bodily forces. We thus remember that there are alternative interpretations to the culturally coded 'figure', interpretations that can be engaged in refusing who we are and becoming something else. There is activity which escapes the completeness of a visual image or the structure of plot. Both emplotment and image construction are only partial descriptions of how selves are and can be constructed. As modes of interpretation they can only include what can be represented in language or culturally coded images. Hence, they are inadequate as an understanding of the complexity of self-construction, and of the variety of ways that technologies of the self operate with and may be complicit with strategies of power. But accounts of self-construction in terms of emplotment and image are also potentially complicit with power strategies themselves. Both the telling of narratives and the making of images can be subversive and experimental, but if we equate them with self-construction they offer a normative expectation that self-construction remains within these confines. As Pollock has pointed out, the 'hypostasized image', which treats what it represents as a concrete reality, promises a completeness or 'wholeness', while narrative offers us 'singular flow of interrelating and mutually reinforcing meaning and positions' (1988: 180). Critique, which can be conducted by art history and by artists themselves, should extend to the roots of this desire and include a suspicion towards the pleasure taken in the completeness or finality of an image or plot.

Thus far, we have discussed how visual art, itself a technology of the self, has a critical role to play in exposing the operation of technologies of the self. The critical work of artists helps to destabilise the rigidity of established modes of subjectivity, and the power structures that they support and emerge from. Visual art thus helps to open up the space for experiments in what it is to be a self. Such experiments will need to include new ways of appearing, moving and inhabiting a space. We need to go beyond critique and develop these alternatives if we are to successfully be untied from our identities. This will involve new explorations and engagement with bodily processes beyond what can be incorporated into cultural narratives and images. To radically challenge existing forms of subjectivity and experiment with new ones will require us to employ technologies which engage the body in a variety of ways, and a hermeneutics of the self which can incorporate multiple processes, and allow for their vicissitudes, rather than trying to confine the self within a plot or complete image. In the next chapter, therefore, I will move from focusing on visual art as a means of critique, which draws attention to visual technologies that contribute to the construction of subjugated subjects, and focus on the possibility of visual art as an exploratory, experimental and creative technology that can contribute to the development of new forms of subjectivity.

NOTE

1. Alan Schrift, C. Colwell and Benda Hofmeyr all note that the possibility of constituting the self differently rests on Foucault's insistence that this constitution is never a purely passive effect of power on the subject but involves the subject's own activity (Colwell 1994; Hofmeyr 2006; Schrift 1995).

5. An Experimental Hermeneutics of the Self

If Foucault is right when he says that the modern subject is a subjugated subject, tied to its own identity in an oppressive and constraining way (Foucault 1982: 781), then what forms could a self that was no longer subjugated take? I have stated before that I do not want to be prescriptive about what form a self should take, but we can still consider what possibilities for selfhood could allow us to respond to the critical concerns discussed in the previous chapter. Here, I think we can usefully compare the different ways a constructed self can relate to identity with Nietzsche's insights into how we can relate to beliefs. Nietzsche attacks fanaticism and the need for convictions, celebrating the contrary. 'Freedom from convictions of any kind, the *capacity* for an unconstrained view *pertains* to strength' (Nietzsche 2005a: 184). But he also criticises an inability to affirm or deny: 'the sceptic, that gentle creature is all too easily frightened. His conscience has been trained to jump at every no, or even at a decisive and hardened yes, and to feel it like a bite' (Nietzsche 2002: 100). He warns us as much of the danger that one cleaves to a sceptical stance as of dogmatically cleaving to one's beliefs. And he calls instead for the need '[n]ot to be stuck in our own detachment' (Nietzsche 2002: 39). What Nietzsche praises instead of either cool detachment or rigid belief is a capacity to embrace, pursue and explore beliefs and values, which provide the framework in which we live and act,[1] combined with the cultivation of an ability to question, move between and ultimately let go of beliefs and values when we need to.[2] My suggestion is that one way to be a non-subjugated self, in contrast to a self that relies on a fixed and rigid identity in their interpretation of experience, actions, etc., would be to be a self who is capable of embracing and employing a particular identity, but who also has the capacity to let go of, or be untied from, this identity, and thus may move between and play with different identities. Identity can be understood in terms of what we take to mark us out as individuals, an answer to the question, as Ricoeur frames it, of 'who did this?' (1988: 246), a question which already interprets the motivating force of various agential drives and activity of automatic bodily processes as cohering in an individual. But identity also connects to broader social and political categories, or group identities such as our gender or class. Identity answers the question of 'who did this?' by picking out a particular individual with a particular character and provides a framework in which we act and understand our actions that can encompass both a particular character and shared group identities. Thus, to be untied from our identity is to accept a fluidity in what we are, which allows us to detach from our existing personal sense of our character, and the patterns of behaviour this may involve, and from the proscribed social and political identities this may incorporate. As well as a capacity to move between and take on different identities, this fluidity might also involve either alternative frameworks of action and interpretation to social and political identities, or very different identities to any we currently find in our cultural library (for instance one that is able to accept a greater degree of diversity, ambiguity and even contradiction). How then, could a more fluid way of relating to oneself be achieved?

Firstly, if Foucault is right when he claims that modern selves are problematically tied to their identity, then they need to be untied. Here criticism is, as explored in the previous chapter, crucial. It allows us to expose the ways in which selves become tied to identities, and particular identities are constructed, and thus to view these identities as contingent. And it exposes the power strategies that both work to deny this contingency and to present particular modes of selfhood as a normative requirement. In the previous chapter, we examined the role that visual art can play in exposing various ways in which the self is continually being constructed and in which we are actively involved in constructing ourselves and others. We saw how narrative is only one among many interpretative practices that contributes to self-construction and emphasised the importance of images as another means by which identity norms are established and often presented as given. We considered, employing Foucault's understanding of power, how such technologies, that work to produce certain kinds of self, operate in the context of particular power regimes and complex power relations, and may work to reinforce those regimes or serve the goals of others. We saw how the identification of a self with particular images or narratives – and the group identities or cultural tropes they are equated with, such as the *femme fatale* or working-class wife – is limiting. But we saw also that the reduction of our identity to images or narratives generally, the assumption that the alternative to a particular identity is always another image or story, can itself be limiting. The example of Cindy Sherman highlighted how we identify women with particular types that we construct using visual cues, but her later work also suggests the presence of bodily processes that are in excess of these culturally coded images. Artworks can gesture towards what is being excluded from existing norms of selfhood. Becoming aware of the ways in which selves are constructed, the role of power, and the exclusions that are effected in establishing particular models or means for self-construction, is a crucial step in opening up the space for new forms of self-construction and in cultivating the self-awareness to avoid simply reproducing the same forms of oppression.

If we are to be untied from our identity we also, however, need to create new identities, or alternative frameworks of interpretation and action that offer alternative modes of selfhood. This requires experimentation and creativity. Here we return to the excess, to the processes that cannot be contained in a story or an image, to what does not fit the mould. Exploring and engaging with the aspects of bodily process and drive activity that are not captured in culturally coded images and narratives can provide resources for this experimentation. A starting point in developing a broader hermeneutics of the self is to explore the processes, and where they can lead, which existing norms of both artistic construction and self-construction work to exclude. Innovation in artistic practice can employ processes that we currently ignore or even expunge, and innovate new hermeneutic practices, thereby making these processes available as resources for self-construction. Art practice can also, however, remind us of the material limits of this experimentation. I am following Foucault in advocating that we work to untie ourselves from the identities that are imposed on us by cultural and social demands and shaped by the power strategies of others. One way this could be achieved is by becoming less attached to any given identity and more able to untie ourselves and move between them. Another is to pursue a more autonomous practice of the hermeneutics of the self, shaping the formation of the identities we attach to according to our own goals, rather than those imposed on us by others, with an accompanying awareness of the workings of power relations and their tendency to induce us to shape ourselves in certain ways. However, I am not suggesting that we, individually or as a cultural group, face no limits to our self-invention. In addition to the fact that we are always operating in the context of a given culture, even as we seek to critique or challenge it, we also, as I stressed in Chapter 3, always operate within the logic of the material processes of our bodies. Further, in addition to exploring potential processes of self-construction, and foregrounding their materiality, artworks can directly contribute to self-construction by engaging and affecting bodily processes through their physical effect on us. Artworks can physically persuade – acting on our senses and our drives to produce physical responses and to influence the direction and interaction of the diverse processes that contribute to our self-construction.

But, as well as the innovation and creation of new identities and modes of being, we need to avoid simply reconstituting a subjugated self that cleaves to its new identities just as rigidly as we did to the old. This will be supported by critical practices that cultivate an awareness of the operation of power, a vigilance against stepping into new traps. Thus, visual art as a critical technology has a role to play not just in opening up space for creativity, as discussed in Chapter 4, but in maintaining it. But this requires more than the critical awareness of the operation of power cultivated by the artworks explored in the previous chapter, it requires a capacity for unlearning and relearning. In this chapter, I will explore artworks that help us do this. Continually breaking habits, unlearning what becomes rigid and ossified, is supported by the cultivation of a playfulness that art can facilitate. To maintain this playfulness and avoid the lure of new traps we also need to encourage in ourselves a capacity for incorporating a diversity of interpretative processes and an ability to move between them. Learning new ways of being implies the need to cultivate new habits, alter the vicissitudes of our drives, develop new muscle memories, which art practice again can facilitate, both by way of example and by way of its physical effects on us.

In this chapter, I want to consider different strategies that artists have employed to go further than the disruption and displacement of dominant images and narratives, to question the completeness of images and narratives and their equation with identity by engaging with processes that they exclude. How have artists explored and engaged the body beyond culture, worked to break habits, cultivate playfulness, and engage drives and other bodily processes, thereby producing new trajectories in them? Artworks that achieve these effects are, or could be taken up as, technologies of self-construction that go beyond criticism and contribute to creating something new. I will first consider the strategy of re-appropriation, considering the example of Claude Cahun as one creative response to critical insights into how cultural images can operate as an oppressive technology. But I will argue that we need to go further than re-appropriating – or even inventing new – images or narratives. Indeed, I think that Cahun's success in escaping from socially proscribed templates for identity comes from her actions and are not reducible to her images. I will consider how various artists, including Yvonne Rainer and Carolee Schneemann, have tried to evade being constituted in terms of an image, by actively stepping out of the frame. I will go on to consider how various artists find opportunities for exploring bodily processes that cannot be captured in a culturally coded figure, by using their own bodies (ORLAN, Carolee Schneemann, Yvonne Rainer, Rebecca Horn), by invoking an absent body (Mona Hatoum), and through the engagement of the audience's body and drives (Marina Abramović, Steve McQueen). I will end by considering how artists may seek not only to reveal but to affect the drives of the spectator (Herman Nitsch). I am not looking to visual art to provide one template for constructing a self, as the novel has been used on the narrative model of selfhood, equating self-construction with the activity of constructing a character in a plot. Rather, visual art offers diverse ways of disrupting existing models of the self and diverse hermeneutic practices that can be incorporated into a plural hermeneutics of the self. It can thus operate as a vital tool in a project of expanding our hermeneutics of the self towards a more diverse practice that embraces its corporeality.

STEPPING OUT OF THE FRAME

One tactic which aims to go beyond the criticism of imagery, both visual and literary, and its role in constructing and also constraining identities, is re-appropriating this imagery. Re-appropriation involves taking control over the images and terms that have been used to subjugate us. This can go beyond the act of self-assertion involved in taking ownership of a particular symbol or term that has been used to denigrate or oppress us. Re-appropriation can involve new interpretations of the meaning of the imagery involved. In the previous chapter, I discussed Meyer's analysis of the use of mirrors in the representation of women in the history of art, and how this imagery reinforced the stigmatisation of women as vain and obsessed with appearance, and potentially the internalisation of this as part of their identity. Mirrors in paintings have served to entrench the norm of women as narcissists, which in turn has worked to undermine their autonomy (Meyers 2002: 114). Meyers continues this discussion with a consideration of women artists who have reclaimed and reconfigured the image of the mirror.

One such artist is the self-named Claude Cahun (née Lucy Schwob). Born in 1894, Cahun was associated with the surrealist movement and her main artistic production made public in her lifetime was her writing. She also produced collage in the surrealist tradition. Cahun was Jewish and identified as a lesbian. With her stepsister and partner Marcel Moore (née Suzanne Moore) she engaged in political resistance to fascism. Cahun and Moore left France for Jersey, and were imprisoned there under Nazi occupation, surviving the Second World War but with a severe cost to their health. In her own life Cahun pushed gender categories with her appearance, cutting her hair short and often dressing in men's clothes, and with her change of name from Lucy to Claude. The photographs that survive her, largely unpublished in her lifetime, sparked a retrospective interest in her work, and in particular in its performative element and the challenge it poses to traditional gender identity. These photographs are labelled as self-portraits but are taken by her partner Moore and might be better viewed as collaborative in authorship (Ades 2017: 176). The series of photographs are intimate, often playful, and defy categorisation according to our expectations of male or female. They include a coquettish image from a series '*I am in Training Don't Kiss Me*' (1927), which blends male and female symbols. In one of the pictures from this series she purses rouged lips while holding weights, her hair short and slicked back, apart from two curls on her forehead, the flatness of her chest highlighted by the black circles over her nipples. More sombre is an earlier portrait, in profile, wearing a man's jacket that mimics a picture of her father and highlights their resemblance (*Self-portrait [in Profile, Wearing Corduroy Jacket]* c. 1919). In others she wears dresses, for example a series in which she dons a plaited blonde wig and an austere expression, performing the role of Elle from the folk tale Blue Beard, who escapes the bloody fate of her predecessors in matrimony (*Self-portrait [Double Head Image as Elle in Barbe-Bleue]*; *Self-portrait [as Elle in Barbe-Bleue]*, 1929). A later series of portraits include Cahun in a peaceful pose, with eyes closed, sun on her face, seated behind a window frame in a feminine playsuit (*Self-portrait [in Window of La Rocquaise]*, 1938). These pictures offer an immense diversity of images but also of possible identities. The photograph that Meyers focuses on in her discussion of the imagery of narcissism is *Self-portrait (Reflected Image in Mirror with Chequered Jacket)* (1928, Figure 5.1). In this brightly lit photograph, Cahun, with short-cropped hair and bronzed skin, poses close to a mirror, making a clear allusion to the Narcissus trope. But she looks not at her reflection in the mirror but out at the viewer, confident and in control. The effect is a doubling in which the persona with a confident gaze that meets ours is different from that of the reflection, whose eyes seem to gaze into the distance with a sense of melancholy, and whose throat is exposed, suggesting vulnerability. Meyers suggests that Cahun's androgynous appearance in this photograph, combined with her look being turned on the viewer of the photograph rather than being directed towards her own reflection, prevents the image from being read as the narcissistic pursuit of beautiful appearance, and thus as continuous with the history of painting women with mirrors. For Meyers:

> Cahun is refiguring the mirror as a self-determination appliance – on the one hand, a repository of inner feelings that the individual sometimes prefers to keep private and, on the other hand, a receptacle for testing out modes of social self-presentation. Abrogating the laws of light refraction, Cahun's pair of mirrors does not create a visual echo chamber that traps her in the psychic/*psyché* economy of feminine narcissism. Together the literature and the metaphorical mirror create a breathing space in which she can experiment with and personalize a novel gendered and sexed look. (Meyers 2002: 140)

Cahun thus takes up the symbol of the mirror and gives it a new meaning, utilising it as a tool of self-determination where it has previously been used as tool of oppression. The woman/mirror imagery is reclaimed and reinterpreted.

Meyers does not suggest we stop with appropriating and giving new meanings to patriarchal imagery. She stresses the importance of 'feminist counterfigurative initiatives' (Meyers 2002: 57). And she demands that feminists should aim at 'fashioning and disseminating emancipatory gender imagery' (Meyers 2002: 192). But the creation of new imagery which Meyers calls for is still not enough. The very possibility of reducing women to an image or a narrative that can be imposed on them has to be disrupted. The power of Cahun's self-portrait comes from far more than her referencing the trope of images of narcissistic women with mirrors, it comes from more than the image itself insofar as we can comprehend it in culturally coded terms. The picture works as a challenge to the stereotype of women as shallow narcissists because the action it testifies to takes it beyond the level of simply quoting the woman/mirror image back at us. Cahun's gaze meets ours, and we feel her presence and her defiance. The photograph also testifies to the varied play with dress, hair and posture that she continually engaged in, and to the challenge her own self-fashioning raised to binary gender identities.

Cahun has been recognised as a precursor of later artists who perform for the camera (Ades 2017: 185). Where Sherman's *Film Stills* quote our cultural language in ways that reveal the reduction of women to coded images, Sherman slipping between different tropes of femininity according to the artifice of the image (which encompasses

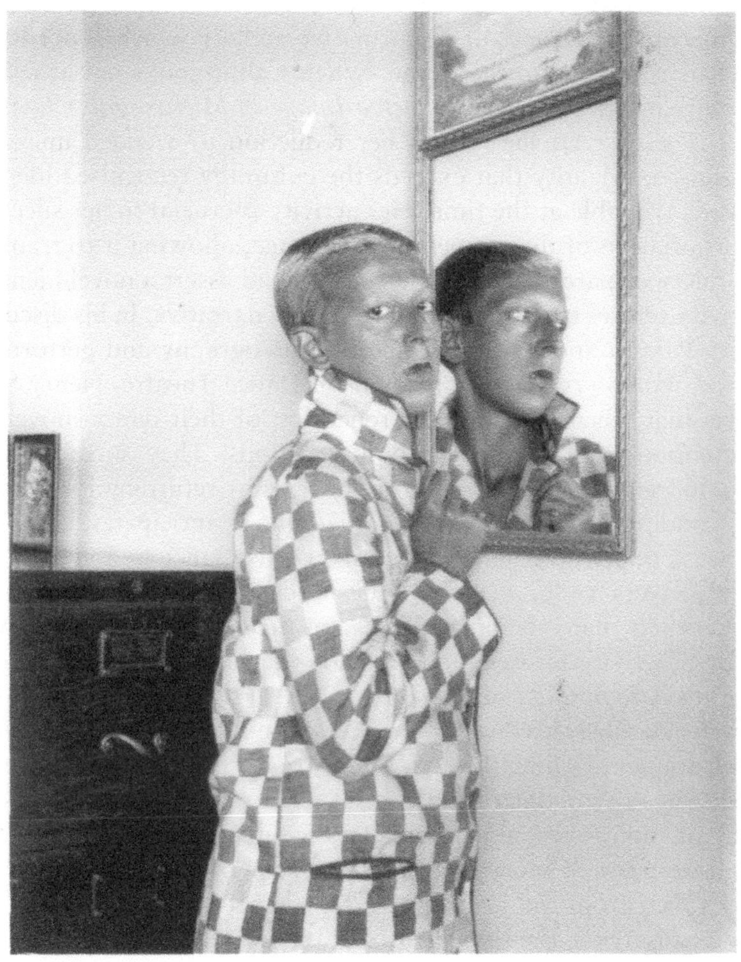

5.1 Claude Cahun, *Self-portrait (Reflected Image in Mirror with Chequered Jacket)*, 1928, gelatin silver print, 25.5 × 20.1 cm. Courtesy of Jersey Heritage Collections

both her costume and make-up and the stylistic markers of the image itself), Cahun refuses to fit into any of the available tropes. Cahun's work looked at as a series of diverse images is witness to her playful experimentation and the creation of alternative identities. She appears sometimes as decidedly feminine, sometime straightforwardly masculine, sometimes utterly androgynous, sometimes as combining elements of the feminine and masculine, but never as a clear type. Cahun wrote

'Masculine? Feminine? It depends on the situation. Neuter is the only gender that always suits me' (Cahun 2007: 151). Moore's photographs of Cahun are thus traces of performative activity which is not limited to what is contained in the frame. When Cahun looks out at us from the picture in *Self-portrait (Reflected Image in Mirror with Chequered Jacket)* (Figure 5.1), she refuses her reduction to a coded image and establishes an identity that exceeds the culturally recognised identities that were available at the time. Her activity is crucial to her successful re-appropriation of the women/mirror image, allowing it to transcend the mimicry of parody or pastiche and instead assert a novel identity.

Activity refuses equation to an image or a narrative. In his discussion of Steve Paxton and Yvonne Rainer's choreography and performance of *Word Words* (1963) with the Judson Dance Theatre, Henry Sayers suggests that when watching the repetition of their dance movements our attention is drawn to the body's actions. They succeed, Sayers argues, in 'removing the body from the gaze by returning it to activity, to the condition of *always doing something*. It anticipates, that is, the role that *acting* will assume in feminist performance by the end of the decade' (Sayers 1989: 118–19). The need to avoid being constituted by others led many feminist artists towards performance, in which their own activity refuses reduction to what can be culturally coded. ORLAN's *Attempting to Escape the Frame with Mask No. 3* (1965), in which she clambers awkwardly, naked and masked, out of the confines of a gilt frame, reaching through the restrictively small round opening, can be seen as symbolic of this refusal. ORLAN is best known for her radical and controversial performances in which she undergoes a series of plastic surgeries, incorporating into her performances standards of beauty taken from the history of art, while remaining conscious and reading from texts, the surgery broadcast to live audiences. This series of works is collectively described as *Re-incarnation of Saint ORLAN* and began in 1990, but it incorporates particular and carefully orchestrated performances. There are various artists, including ORLAN and Stelarc, whose work includes, though is not reducible to, an exploration of the implications of medical technologies. My focus in this book is on the myriad ways in which self-construction is always occurring and can occur, and specifically the limits of a narrative theory as an account of this hermeneutic process. My concern is to argue that visual art broadly construed can help us explore and expand our understanding and practice of a hermeneutics of the self. This can of course incorporate developments in information and medical technology, and these can be seen as continuous with artworks operating as technologies of the self, which modify the body through, for example, the cultivation of new habits. However, I have made the decision that to adequately enter into the complexity of the debates that radical modifications through modern technologies – employing for example robotics, implants or genetic modifications – open up around what constitutes the human or posthuman is too much of a diversion from my focus in this book. The use I wish to make of the example of ORLAN here, therefore, leaves untouched various questions her work raises in relation to the latter topic. In ORLAN's evolving and controversial performances she both disrupts iconic imagery of beautiful women, such as Botticelli's Venus and Da Vinci's *Mona Lisa*, and refuses to become an image herself. Conscious and performing as she undergoes surgery, continually changing her own physical appearance in a series of operations, not only is ORLAN refusing reduction to an image she also refuses reduction to appearance by making her appearance mutable.

Carolee Schneemann explicitly refers to the motivation of avoiding passive constitution in discussing her work. Schneemann, who saw herself fundamentally as a painter, and who 'enlarged her canvas' using happenings and performance, declared the need to use 'live body action' because film 'permits the passive viewing' (Schneemann 1997: 32, 236).[3] Schneemann suggests that the use of her body in her artwork challenged the assumption that she 'WAS PERMITTED TO BE AN IMAGE/BUT NOT AN IMAGE-MAKER CREATING HER OWN SELF-IMAGE' (Schneemann 1997: 194). Schneemann's extensive performance work includes *Meat Joy* (1963) – a group performance which builds to the ecstatic contortions, interactions and piling up of eight naked bodies smeared with paint and raw meat, which Schneemann herself claims had 'the character of an erotic rite: excessive indulgent, a celebration of flesh as material' (Schneemann 1997: 63) – and the solo performance *Interior Scroll* (1975), in which she reads from a scroll that she pulls out from her vagina. The later performance she repeated as an action in 1977 at the Telluride film festival in order to 'stand out step out of frame' (Schneemann 1997: 237). Thus, for women artists, one pull to performance, of, as Sayers puts it, returning to activity, was that it offered a means of taking control and escaping the framed image, refusing passive constitution by others. Replacing an image of the body with the body itself does not, as I will discuss below, evade the problem of objectification, and the body of the female artist is still subject to the male gaze. Perhaps Sayers's claim that we *remove* the body from the gaze through activity is too strong, but in their activity Rainer, Paxton, ORLAN and Schneemann all refuse to let themselves be held in the gaze, to be fixed as an image or constituted by it. Their work can thus be viewed as practices that refuse constitution by the

    Visual Art and Self-Construction

other and thus as contributing to a hermeneutics of the self that aims at a non-subjugated self.

Performance art that employs the body, however, is more than an escape act, dodging being trapped by an objectifying eye. For many artists, performance also aimed to engage, for both artist and audience, 'new ranges of emotion' (Sayers 1989: 95). Performance art hopes to open up new perspectives on the body by using the body in novel ways and engaging the body of the audience. How can artworks operate as experimental technologies of the self which not only evade constitution by an objectifying gaze that images are subject to, but which also allow us to incorporate into our hermeneutics of the self that which images exclude? In the next section, I want to consider a variety of artworks including but not limited to performance, which explore different perspectives on the body and induce new bodily experiences in the viewers. They can thereby hope to engage, and make available to our hermeneutics of the self, bodily practices in excess of the codification of image or narrative. In this way, visual art can act as a technology of the self which can discover and explore but also affect bodily processes.

HARNESSING THE EXCESS

In speaking of the motivation behind her series of tableaux, *Eye Body: 36 Transformative Actions for Camera* (1963), constructed using her own naked body combined with other materials such as paint and feathers, Schneemann says she sought 'to "conceive" of my body in manifold aspects which had eluded the culture around me' (Schneemann 1997: 52). How can we express and engage bodily processes that elude culture; the excess that refuses the mould, the 'something' beyond representability that we have seen is gestured towards by Bacon and Sherman, who employ but also disrupt the figure? One tactic is to invoke the body without figurative representation. The figure operates within a cultural visual language, even when pushed to its limits, as with Bacon. Employing the body without figurative representation is an opportunity to explore bodily processes without the coding that figurative art inevitably involves.

One way that I think figurative representation of the body, and thus its reduction to codes, can be avoided is through the use of actual bodies, as in performance work that uses the body, such as Schneemann's aforementioned group performance *Meat Joy* (1963). Amelia Jones notes the concern that the presence of the female body is '*necessarily* participating in the phallocentric dynamic of fetishism', which led feminist artists such as Mary Kelly to exclude the body from any visible presence in their work (Jones 1998: 24). But as Jones argues, it is not inevitable that the body remains purely a 'fetish object for a pleasure seeking male gaze' (1998: 27). As Berger suggests 'the nude is always conventionalized – and the authority for its conventions derives from a certain tradition of art' but '[a] naked body has to be seen as an object in order to become a nude' (Berger 1972: 53, 54). The artist can challenge the audience to engage in alternative ways of relating which do not involve turning the artist into an object. At the same time, Jones cautions against viewing body art, which she understands as performance and multimedia art that uses the artist's body, as delivering an unmediated body to the viewer (1998: 33). I think Jones is right both to assert on the one hand the radical possibilities of an artist using their own body, refusing the assumption that the reception of body art is predictable and fixed within our existing problematic ways of seeing and interpreting, and to also insist that this body is never a 'whole' that offers up a final meaning. It is this completeness of identity that images and narratives promise us, and normatively insist on, that the body of the artist can disrupt through activity. However, when Jones asserts the incompleteness of the meaning of the body artwork, it is because any meaning for her is ultimately dependent on the interpretative context in which the viewer interacts with it. Certainly, the artist, even while refusing passivity, does not have complete control over the reception of their work, and with body art the interpretation of their body. But while I agree with Jones's emphasis on intersubjectivity as integral to the effects of live performance, and with her insistence on the incompleteness of meaning, I reject the claim that 'the body art work only has meaning in virtue of its contextualization within the codes of identity that accrue to the artist's name/body' (Jones 1998: 34). This is to remain too closely aligned to a textual understanding of hermeneutics, in which the body, or any artwork, stands in for the book. Jones uses a Derridean framework to liberate the body artwork from authorial determination, insisting rather on the open-ended creation of meaning in the interpretative encounter with the reader/viewer. But I think artists can engage the body in ways that are not subsumed by codes of identity. The use of the body in an artwork allows us to explore the interpretative processes that the body itself is continually engaged in, and which elude representational convention. Interpretation does, as Jones reminds us, always operate in an intersubjective and cultural context, but it is not limited to what can be 'read' off the work, it is already occurring in processes of bodily activity and artistic creation.

Performance artists have often experimented with their own and other performers' bodies, for instance Schneemann suggests in her notes that '[t]he voice expresses pressures of the total musculature so that we may discover unique sounds possible during specific physical actions' (Schneemann 1997: 10). She states further that this exploration of what the body can do, how the body will be affected, is crucially 'not a predictable, predetermined process' (Schneemann 1997: 10). Performance art that uses the body thus provides an opportunity to explore the potential of bodily processes to experience and enter into new perspectives on the body. It can be seen as an experiment in the materiality of the body, exploring its possibilities and its horizons, the logic of its inherent processes, the extent to which the trajectory of these processes can deviate, and the limit of its plasticity. If the body is not treated as fixed, offered in its presence as complete, but is rather recognised to be mutable, open to new interpretations and engaged itself in forming new interpretations, then its activity can be a means of exploring it potentialities and creating new and multiple meanings. We do not have to accept either Pollock's view that the female body cannot be employed in art because it will always be determined by an objectifying gaze, nor the fetishisation of presence which Jones cautions against, if we remember that the body is never static. Rather, in bodily activity, as Sayers emphasises in his discussion of Paxton and Rainer, we find a refusal of any single or final interpretation because activity exceeds any fixed interpretation.

The exploration of the body, and the potential interpretations it can generate, applies to the bodies of the audience as well as the body of the performer. For Schneemann, her performance works are extensions of her painting-constructions, though the:

> force of a performance is necessarily more aggressive and immediate in its effect [. . .] the spectator is overwhelmed with changing recognitions, carried emotionally by a flux of evocative actions and led or held by the specified time sequence which marks the duration of the performance. (Schneemann 1997: 10)

While Schneemann suggests that we are more active visually if looking at a painting, construction or sculpture, she claims that '[d]uring a theater piece the audience may become more active *physically*' and:

> their physical reactions will tend to manifest *actual* scale—relating to motions, mobilities the body does make in a *specific* environment. They maybe have to act, to do things, to assist some activity, to get out of the way, to dodge or catch falling objects. They enlarge their kinaesthetic field of participation; their attention is required by a varied span of actions, some of which may threaten to encroach on the integrity of their positions in space. (Schneemann 1997: 10)

The proximity of the audience is crucial to the effect of Schneemann's work and that of other performance artists. With *Meat Joy*, for example, 'the audience were seated on the floor as close to the performance as possible' (Schneemann 1997: 63). According to Schneemann the audience of a performance or happening 'may find their bodies performing on the basis of immediate visual circumstances [. . .] at the same time their senses are heightened by the presence of human forms in action and by the temporality of the actions themselves' (Schneemann 1997: 10). Thus, discovery concerning the body's possibilities concerns the audience's interactions with and reactions to the performance as well as the performer's experiments with their own bodily functions and capacities.

If artworks are going to operate as technologies of the self that can reveal, engage and affect bodily processes and drives, pursuing their potential beyond the limits of cultural norms, then they need to induce us to take new perspectives on the body, and open up new ways of experiencing our bodies. One artist who achieves this is Rebecca Horn with her sculptural body extensions, which she describes as allowing her to 'perform certain experiments upon myself' (Haenlein 1997: 16). For example, within the film *Performances II* (1972), Horn wears gloves with metre-long black extensions to her fingers, which she calls *Handschuhfinger* (Finger Gloves). These prostheses, fashioned from wood and fabric, simultaneously extend and restrict her bodily capacity. She can reach further with her extended fingers than with her bare hands. The gloves are light and easy to move, and she can grasp objects and touch with them. She is, however, isolated from the world when she wears them and distanced from the objects that she touches with them. Horn claims that she abandoned using her own body in her art because these experiments remained in the 'the realm of personal experience' (Haenlein 1997: 16). However, I think the film footage, and to an extent the artefact of the gloves themselves, and the photographic image of Horn wearing the gloves (Figure 5.2), render tangible for us the significance of tactile connection to our interpretation of the world. The importance of the haptic is registered through the interference that gloves interject into our normal tactile relationship with objects. There is still touch; Horn even suggests that 'the lever action of the lengthened fingers intensifies the sense of touch in the hand' (Haenlein 1997: 58). But this touch is mediated by the material of the gloves and the distance they create. It is an unfamiliar touch. It thereby physically reminds us of tactility as a mode of interpretation that can contribute to self-constructions, prompting us to pay attention to the significance of tactile sensation. As Lynne Cooke suggests with Finger Gloves 'sight

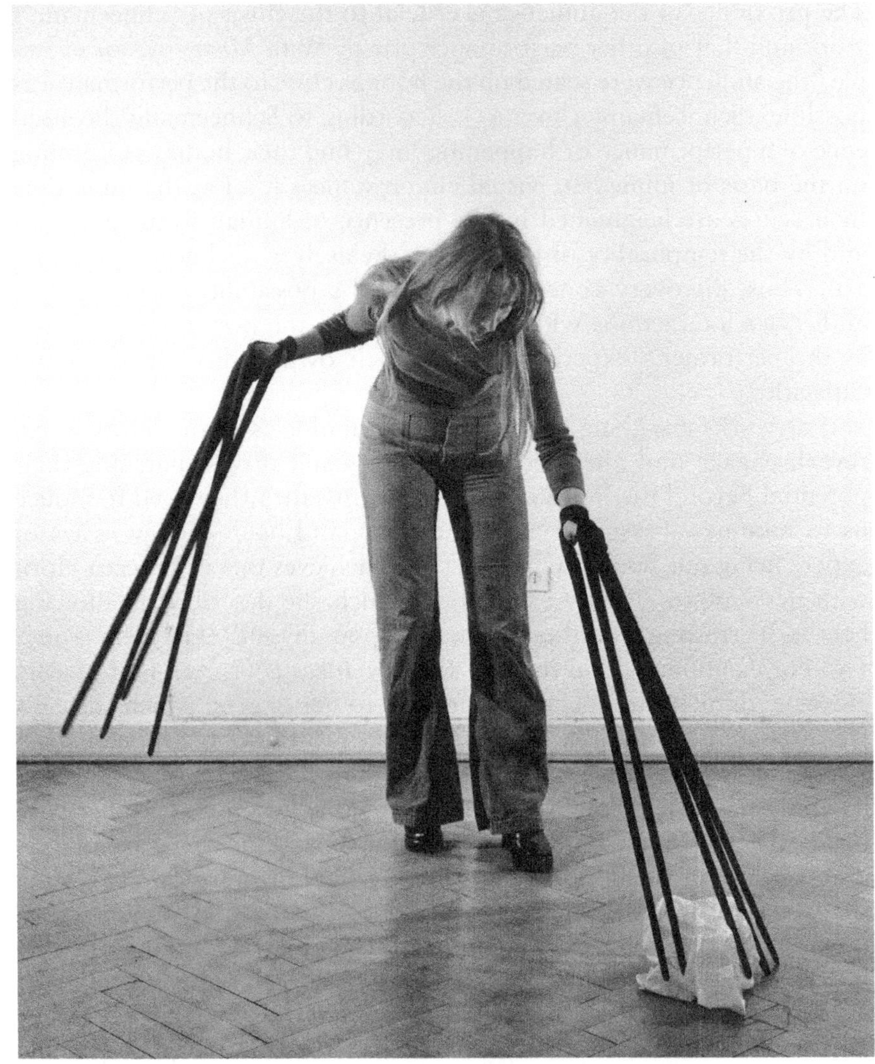

5.2 Rebecca Horn, *Finger Gloves*, 1972, Performance 2, fabric, balsa wood, length 90cm. Photographer: Achim Thode. © Rebecca Horn/VG Bild Kunst/ DACS, 2020. Credit: Tate, London – with the help of the Tate Members, 2002

cedes to touch in firmly locating, grounding and positioning the self in the world' (Haenlein 1997: 23). Horn's experiment makes us aware of tactile modes of interpretation that already play a role in shaping the kind of self that we are and permits us the option of giving greater emphasis to, or directing this form of interpretation towards, particular goals of self-construction and reconstruction. It thus expands the interpretations that we can incorporate into our hermeneutics of the self.

Yvonne Rainer's work, in which she choregraphs task like repetitive action, also gives a new perspective on the body and its potential. For instance, in the dance *Trio A* (choreographed in 1966 and filmed in 1978), we see a flow of movements: bending, swaying, squatting, kneeling, rolling, standing and lying down. Watching it we become of aware of the effect of rhythm and gravity on the body. Also, with its lack of any music, we witness the specificity of the rhythm of different bodies, as when the dance is performed together by more than one dancer the duration varies between them (Bryan-Wilson 2012: 54). We sense that the dancer's movements have their own logic and impetus, conserving energy, or expressing forces. Through engaging with Rainer's artwork, we come to understand that movement is another mode of interpretation, and thus provides another possibility of self-construction within a corporeal hermeneutics of the self that incorporates multiple interpretations.

The interconnectedness of bodily movement and our sense of self has been highlighted by Iris Marion-Young in her seminal essay 'Throwing Like a Girl' from 1980, which discusses the gender differences in movement and the occupation of space (Marion-Young 1990). Her starting point is Erwin Straus's observations of the differences between how even very young boys and girls approach throwing a ball differently. The girl does not employ her whole body in the way that a boy does. But this, Strauss acknowledges, cannot be explained through physiological sexual difference. Marion-Young expands this to consider more widely the differences in movement and style of women's and men's bodies:

> Even in the most simple body orientations of men and women as they sit, stand and walk, one can observe a typical difference in body style and extension. Women generally are not as open with their bodies as men are in their gait and stride. Typically, the masculine stride is longer proportional to a man's body than is the feminine stride to a women's. The man typically swings his arms in a more open and loose fashion [. . .] Women tend not to put their whole bodies into engagement in a physical task with the same ease and naturalness as men. (1990: 145)

Marion-Young thus notes how bodily movements are interactive with gender identity (which in turn is part of a particular identity that a self is more or less tied to).

What does Rainer's *Trio A* add to this analysis? Julia Bryan-Wilson, in reflecting on *Trio A*, considers the nature of dance practice:

> There is something in dance called 'muscle memory'—the capturing of movement within your flesh so thoroughly that when you move, you can do so without much conscious thinking. The body can contain and store thought, history and meaning; it is capable of holding and learning and even teaching the mind. (2012: 69–70)

Trio A shows us then, how, through muscle memory, various patterns of interpretation – how we swing our arms, how we stride, how we throw, etc. – which may support and express particular identities, are established.

Schneemann suggests that if she had 'only been dancing, acting' she 'would have maintained forms of feminine expression acceptable to the culture' (Schneemann 1997: 194). But she was also directing the theatrical productions that she performed in and thus creating new forms of expression, while Rainer choregraphs a radically different kind of dance expanding its vocabulary from established gendered expressions. Hence, as a choreographed dance performed by different dancers *Trio A* demonstrates not just how gestures and patterns of movement that follow culturally acceptable lines form, but also the possibility of unlearning these patterns, and establishing new interpretations of movement. Schneemann, reflecting on her group performance works, claims that while their character depends on spontaneous movement and gesture, 'each particular work took a great deal of training for us to reach a fluid physical inter-relation that isn't inherently part of our culture' (Schneemann 1997: 184). If we can train ourselves to unlearn patterns of moving and relating, then we create space for new gestures and movement, and develop new muscle memories that break with culturally established forms. Of the dancers she works with Schneemann says 'their bodies are capable of feats', from a tradition of movement that their body knows, they must reach towards 'the forms which they must search to break clear of past traditions' (Schneemann 1997: 17). Rainer's and Schneemann's artworks thus provide us with examples of how new bodily interpretations can be developed that do not conform to the bodily expressions that express, and work to tie us to, our existing culturally established identities.

At the same time a work such as Rainer's *Trio A* makes us aware that new interpretations, the cultivation of new muscle memories, must work with the material of the body, the body's weight and susceptibility to gravity, its flexibility and range of movement have to be expanded gradually and ultimately have their limits; joints have a maximum rotation, muscles can only be stretched so far without injury. Just as Louise Bourgeois observed how the materials of her sculptures both pushed into new concerns and presented resistances, the body has its own tendencies of movement and limits of plasticity. *Trio A* can teach us about the possibility and limitations of movement as a mode of interpretation that can be incorporated into the multiple practices that contribute to our self-construction. Thus, it is an example of how performances which use the body can explore bodily processes that escape figurative representation, allowing us to inhabit new perspectives. Learning from *Trio A*, we can start to experiment with where these processes can take us and with what ways they can contribute to a hermeneutics of the self that does not merely reproduce oppressive forms of subjectivity. But Rainer's piece is also an example of how artworks must experiment with the body in a way that is sensitive to the trajectories and limits of bodily process. Hence, Schneemann's desire in her artistic endeavours for a dance in which the dancers 'are aware of the impulse, the necessity by which they move and its implicit diminution or contrary flow' (Schneemann 1997: 18). Thus, the search for new movements and forms cannot be a rupture but a gradual retraining and development that still works with our underlying corporeality. Just as a sculptor must develop a feeling for the vicissitudes of their material, working with the 'fundamental life of any material' they use (Schneemann 1997: 9), the artist who works with the body develops a feel for its various processes, and their pliability or intransience, and thus offers us a resource for understanding the materiality of our self-construction.

These examples of work by Schneemann, Horn and Rainer are all performances which employ the artist's body. They all illustrate that artworks can be employed by us as technologies of the self that allow us to unlearn patterns of bodily interpretation, develop new experimental interpretations and engage in play in trying out different interpretations. They do this through the bodily activity of the artist, as well as the bodily effects of the work on its audience. But the body can also be invoked in its absence. In many of the Palestinian artist Mona Hatoum's pieces the body is not present but it is intimated. In an interview with Janine Antoni, Hatoum suggests of her own work that '[t]he sculptures based on furniture are very much about the body', we encounter a body that is not there and 'they encourage the viewer to mentally project him or herself onto the object' (Archer et al. 2016: 143). An example is the disturbing *Day Bed* (2008), a scaled-up grater which both invites that one recline on it, with its chaise-lounge like proportions and shape, and at the same time with its sharp surface prohibits it, reminding us of the vulnerability of our flesh.

Hatoum's use of familiar furniture and objects that we associate with the domestic sphere evokes bodily presence through absence. The body is the missing element suggested by the expectation of our habitual interactions with and reliance on these objects. The body's interconnection with objects, the way they extend its powers, but also the way we desire them and attach to them, is thus one perspective that Hatoum brings to light. Her works using household objects, for example the electrified kitchen implements in *Home* (1999), employ the familiar in uncomfortable new contexts that emphasise danger and alienation. The use of objects we might associate with home, family and comfort makes their subversion all the more disturbing and threatening. Hatoum wants the body of the audience to interact with her artworks, claiming that the aim is that 'the viewer is somehow implicated or even visually or psychologically entrapped in some of the installations' (Archer et al. 2016: 143). This is the case for instance with *The Light at the End* (1989). The piece consists of six red, hot bars emitting heat and red light at the end of a dark narrowing space. From a distance the viewer sees six red lines in the dark, but as they approach they experience the heat of the bars, a physical warning, transmitted sensually, not to come too close. Guy Brett describes his personal experience of the artwork:

> The moment of transition from optical to bodily sensation was an unforget-table experience, a kind of Zen *satori*. Light changed to heat and the visual sense was perturbed and enlarged by the sense of the body as a whole, arousing a disturbing complex of feelings. Attraction to the warmth was mixed with fear. The barrier appeared to be permeable but associated with great risk and danger. At that moment the habitual connection of the eye with detachment and distance was challenged. It became almost physically impossible simply to 'look on' in a state of neutrality, and you felt yourself responsible for your actions. (Archer et al. 2016: 60, 63)

Brett's own body is affected by his engagement with the artwork and he is brought to a new understanding through this bodily experience. He experiences an interconnection between his senses and his emotional reactions and drives. This allows him to achieve an understanding, at the level of bodily experience not abstract theory, that vision is a bodily perspective rather than an objective and distanced mode of contemplation. As Nietzsche would have it 'an eye where the active and interpretative powers are to be suppressed, absent, but through which seeing still becomes a seeing-something' is 'an absurdity' (Nietzsche 2007: 87). With *The Light at the End*, the interpretation of the eye that sees the bars of red lights comes to incorporate the interpretation of the senses that feel the heat, and that of the drives that attract and repel us towards this heat. Engaging with this piece asserts the interconnection of different modes of bodily interpretation and militates against both the privilege of vision and its distortion into the absurdity of a neutral and objective gaze. It is thus an instance of an artwork working to show us the presence of multiple interpretations and the potential of incorpo-rating them in their interactions, both symbiotic and antagonist, as part of our hermeneutics of the self.

With Hatoum's *Corps Étranger* (1994) the body is once again present, filmed in its interiority with an endoscopic camera, but not subverting the conventions of representation and clearly not offered as a figure. Tracey Warr and Amelia Jones claim that by turning the body inside out Hatoum challenges the construction of the body as 'codifiable' and thus '"possessable or exchangeable"' (Warr and Jones 2000: 42). The viewer is swallowed up in the footage of Hatoum's own body. Hatoum describes this work, an installation that incorporates footage of her own insides, thus:

> There is basically one sweeping shot surveying the surface of the body in extreme close-up in a claustrophobic way. We then follow the camera as it penetrates inside the body through various orifices into the stomach intestines, vagina . . . I wanted to give the feeling that the body becomes vulnerable in the face of the scientific eye, probing it, invading its boundaries, objectifying it . . . on the other hand when you enter the room, in places, you feel like you are on the edge of an abyss that can swallow you up, the devouring womb, the vagina dentata, castration anxiety. (Archer et al. 2016: 131)

It is a work that extends Hatoum's long-standing interest in surveillance. It involves a Foucauldian critique of visibility and examination, the camera violating the last vestiges of our body: its interior, the gallery-goer invading this space, literally treading on it, when they enter into the installation. But it also involves a new experience of the body. Warr and Jones suggest the experience of this installation is such that '[o]ur desire to present ourselves (our bodies) as coherent containers of our chosen identity is thwarted through our identification with the mucoid tunnels beneath' (Warr and Jones 2000: 42). We are reminded of the hidden orifices, fluids and processes that culture would have us forget. Self-construction that would exclude this continual bodily activity of swallowing, digesting, secreting is revealed to be a self-construction based on denial, which seeks a sanitised and artificially complete identity in place of the fluid processes that may invoke disgust. We are reconnected with the excess of bodily process that image or plot excludes.

Installations allow artists to play on the potential of artworks to affect our senses and our bodies in different ways and engineer bodily experiences in the audience members. Steve McQueen's film *Bear* (1993) for instance depends on the controlled conditions of its viewing for its full effect. *Bear* projects a black and white film of two naked black men, one McQueen, sparring but also smiling and winking, the mood shifting between threat and flirtation. Due to the size of the screen and the close-up shots the wrestling, dancing, shifting figures are larger than the viewer. The polished floor of the gallery reflects the image, ensuring the viewers implication in the scene. McQueen says of the work:

> Projecting the film on to the back wall of the gallery space so that it com-
> pletely fills it from ceiling to floor, and from side to side, gives it this kind
> of blanket effect. You are very much involved with what is going on. You
> are a participant, not a passive viewer. The whole idea of making it a silent
> experience is so that when people walk into the space they become very
> much aware of themselves, of their own breathing. (Bickers 1996: 2)

The different angles, the larger-than-life size of the bodies on screen, and
the silence allow the audience to take a new perspective on the bodies of
the two men acting in the film, but also to experience their own body as
viewers. We are, as McQueen himself says, aware of our own breathing
when we engage with this work. McQueen succeeds in his aim to make
the audience aware of the movements and processes of their bodies,
of their physicality. But I would add that the audience also become
aware of their desires. In the previous chapter, we saw how Sherman's
Film Stills give the viewer a critical awareness of the way in which we
as viewers construct the identity of the various women she dresses up
as, according to the cultural types the given image suggests to us. In
these early works, Sherman addressed the active role of the viewer in
the constitution of the identity of women and their objectification. But
McQueen gives us an awareness of ourselves as more than viewers,
we feel ourselves as living, breathing, desiring, sensual and corporeal.
We are bodies looking at, responding to, bodies, though inevitably
bodies that have a cultural reality which includes the interpretative
frameworks of race, sexuality and gender. As with Hatoum's work, the
idea of vision as independent of other modes of interpretation is again
undermined. We are forced to confront that all modes of interpretation,
including vision and desire, interact. This awareness, achieved through
engaging with a work of art, thus opens up new possibilities for incorporating a range of interpretations into our hermeneutics of the self.

LIVING IN OUR DRIVES

I began this book by considering the different reactions invoked
by Goya's *Disaster of War* prints. In Chapter 1, I considered how
Nietzsche and Freud's theory of drives explained the multiplicity of
interpretations active in the moment of encountering an artwork. We
also saw how the complexity of our experience of artworks, and the
account of this in terms of a multiplicity of active drives, presents a
challenge to the idea of a unified self. I have argued that the self should
be understood as formed through various interpretative processes and
practices and contingently uniting this diversity. The theory that the self
incorporates a multiplicity of drives providing different interpretations

and impetuses to act challenges the idea that we can equate the self with a simple, conscious agency. This, as discussed in Chapter 3, requires that we rethink our understanding of the agency of self-construction. It presents a challenge for projects in which we want to direct our self-construction towards particular goals and forces us to accept that any such trajectory may be subject to competing demands. The idea that the agency of self-construction could be multiple, sometimes unconscious, with shifting collaborations and loci of dominance, however, opens up possibilities, as well as challenges, for projects of self-cultivation and self-transformation that we may undertake as part of our hermeneutics of the self. It allows for a diversity of technologies of the self affecting us at various levels, which need not be conscious and which can contribute to our self-construction, self-cultivation and reconstruction.

Various artists deliberately explore and seek to engage and affect the drives. In defending body art, Jones argues that the critical strategy of distanciation advocated by Pollock is not the only way artworks can be politically critical and radical. Distanciation aims to induce the active participation of the viewer through tactics of defamiliarisation, which thus 'liberate the viewer from the state of being captured by the illusion of art' (Pollock 1988: 163). By contrast, Jones argues that 'body art practices solicit rather than distance the spectator', but eliciting pleasure does not preclude the active participation of the audience in the development of new interpretations and ways of relating to each other (Jones 1998: 31). Schneemann's work, for example, can be seen to incite pleasure and engage our libidinal drives, but why should this be limited to reproducing the desiring male gaze rather than exploring alternative forms and manifestations of desire? Assuming that is that we are armed with a critical awareness of the desiring male gaze, and its internalisation by women, which various visual artists, as discussed in the previous chapter, have equipped us with. Schneemann claimed that '[a]lienation from our physical joys, constrictions in the scope of our own physical natures, meant endless disasters, acts against our own deepest needs' (Schneemann 1997: 194). Schneemann thus positioned her celebration of the libidinal, involving the seduction of the viewer, as potentially liberating. Her work conceived thus, works on us and potentially changes its audience by working on their drives.

Artworks can operate as technologies that engage the drives on two levels. Firstly, as I discussed above, in terms of expanding perspectives on the body and its processes it makes us aware of bodily processes such as drive activity and thus makes this activity a potential resource in our deliberate self-experimentation. Artworks can help us to fulfil the task that Nietzsche sets us: 'to look into the world through as *many* eyes as possible, to *live in* drives and activities *so as* to create eyes for ourselves' (Nietzsche 1988: vol. 9, 494–5). In various ways artworks can enable us to inhabit and explore the drives. Some performance artists have gone further than stimulating and provoking the drive reactions of their audience and invite the audience to express drives in actions. Yoko Ono's *Cut Piece* (1964) instructed the audience to cut away pieces of her clothing with scissors. Going further, Marina Abramović's infamous *Rhythm O* (1974) invited the audience to use any of 72 objects laid out on a table 'as desired', with Abramović positioning herself as 'the object'. This performance in Naples lasted six hours. The objects chosen could produce pleasure, pain or even death, and included a feather, bandage, soap, saw, whip, knife and a gun. Her clothes were cut off, her skin cut, the gun was aimed at her, other audience members intervened. The audience were allowed to caress her or harm her. The performance demonstrated the presence of sadistic and violent drives, operating as a shocking revelation of their continual activity and potency. The participants explored drives in their activity. Thus, artworks can furnish us with a greater awareness of the interpretative activity of our drives in both breadth and depth, allowing us to become more aware of the diversity of drives and thus the range of perspectives they establish, and enabling us to inhabit and live in particular drives. Artworks can thereby expand the interpretations that we are able to incorporate as part of our hermeneutics of the self, which can employ a range of technologies in the interpretative process of self-construction.

Secondly, in addition to exposing and exploring drives, artworks can also hope to affect the trajectories of the drives, for instance by providing them with new objects, which in turn affects their character, or with new possibilities for expression and release. In Chapter 1 we noted that Freud added to our understanding of drives the important recognition that the objects that drives are directed towards, including other people, affect their trajectory and the character of these drives. Artworks can themselves operate as objects for our drives, modifying them in the process.

An artist who goes to extreme lengths with the aim of providing a release for drives that are otherwise suppressed in civilised society is the Austrian artist Herman Nitsch. Nitsch's work makes reference to both Dionysiac and Christian rites in his ritualistic and dramatic performances, employing for instance the crucifix, animal sacrifice and frenzied dance. Intense, loud music, naked actors, gutted animal carcases, the ripping apart of flesh, all feature. Between 1962 and 2020 Nitsch has staged multiple performances as part of his *Orgien*

Mysterien Theater (OMT). The most extensive of these is the 100th action, *6-Tage-Spiel*, a six-day performance in 1998 at his estate in Prinzendorf, involving 100 actors and 180 musicians. Actions were spread out across the estate and viewers had no fixed schedule. Susan Jarosi notes that Nitsch's work involves a 'conspicuous consideration of audience' and aims to produce 'intensified registration of sensation' and 'catharsis' (Jarosi 2013).[4]

Discussing his work, we come head to head with a problem of writing about performance art generally. If the effect of the work depends on its proximity and immediacy as live performance, then reports, videos and photographs will always be inadequate to convey the experience for the audience. Given Nitsch's emphasis on an immersive experience and sensory overload this is particularly pertinent in considering his work. It is necessary therefore to appeal to subjective descriptions by those, such as Jarosi, who have been present at his OMT events. She describes one of the actions in the six-day play as follows:

> On the afternoon of the second day, for example, the major action staged in the courtyard comprised a series of vignettes that layered elements of religious ritual and mythological narrative [. . .] This action engaged the participation of all the actors and assistants and every musician; audience members could approach the proceedings from any angle, but were never permitted to participate directly. Nitsch orchestrated the events, directing his chief assistant, who in turn supervised actors assigned to undertake either 'passive' or 'active' tasks, which served as metaphors for contrasting states of being: passive performers remained inert, tied to crosses, blindfolded, often naked, and subject to actions such as being inundated with blood and draped with entrails; active performers transported the bound actors, poured the blood and rent the entrails, and also smashed and stomped on grapes and tomatoes [. . .] The effect was of choreographed chaos, produced from highly structured, programmed, and precisely executed tasks characterized by dynamic excess and frenzy. The string orchestra, the heurige band, and the church bells played raucously; the synthesized sounds droned incessantly; sirens blared, bodies milled, geese ran about. (Jarosi 2013: 836–7)

Jarosi describes her own 'immersive experience' as involving a range of competing responses, which included an instinctive flight reaction (Jarosi 2013: 858). Nitsch's emphasis in describing his work is on a release or working through of drives in the context of sensory overload or orgiastic frenzy (Jarosi 2013: 843). Nitsch's website describes the OMT as 'comparable to psychoanalysis', thus Nitsch's explicit aim, in line with Jarosi's presentation of his work, is to work on and release repressed drives, and, as stated on the website, to render viewable the repressed. Nitsch states that the 'technique of the play helps us' in 'plumbing to the depths of the reality of our drives, usually remaining uncharted territory. repressed areas are unearthed and lived out' (Nitsch n.d., a). But crucially this is an aesthetic process which recognises the bodily nature of the drives, and thus engages them through sensual and physical experience. Nitsch states that the OMT's effect on the drives works through the 'sensory sensations evoked by the actions, which, once the censors are overcome, disinhibit and intoxicate' (Nitsch n.d., a).

Further, the aim of the work goes beyond the individual cure of neurosis and hopes to induce in us a new experience of the world in which 'the rapturous intensity of existence must spread over all areas of being, across everyday life. a world overcome with cheerful joviality should allow us to serenely immerse in all possibilities of enjoyment. all the senses have to be intensified and sensitized', which echoes Nietzsche's call for a gay or joyful science (Nietzsche 2001; Nitsch n.d., a). Nitsch's work can thus be seen as a technology, he himself describes it as an instrument (Nitsch n.d., b), which has the potential both to expose the multiplicity of our drive interpretations and allow us to '*live in*' them as Nietzsche advocates, but also to work directly on the vicissitudes of our drives allowing repressed complexes to be worked through, and drives to find new forms of expression. Nitsch self-consciously positions his art as a form of communal therapy and thus as a technology of the self that acts directly on our drives. It is thus an example of the possibility of artworks not only modelling and exploring processes, including drive activity, that contribute to our self-construction, but affecting and alternating these processes and thus the self that is being constructed.

CONCLUSION

The artworks discussed in this chapter invite us to inhabit new perspectives, exposing and affecting our bodily processes. These processes encompass the operation of our senses, muscle memory, gesture and drive activity. In doing so they both reveal the myriad of bodily interpretations that can contribute to our self-construction and act on these interpretative processes. As the artist Joseph Beuys says, 'every person continually performs material processes' (Beuys 2004: 21). Artworks make us aware of and affect these processes. They thus operate as experimental technologies of the self. They take us beyond the important work of criticism, which reveals both the ways in which the self is constructed in the context of power relations and the contingency of the normative standards of self-construction. The artworks discussed in this chapter show us that artworks can go beyond criticism and assist us in the task of unlearning habits and reactions and of developing new ways of interpreting.

The artists I have focused on this chapter emphasise the effect of their work on the body of the audience, they see the interpretation of their work as involving the physical reactions of the viewer. With Ono and Abramović the audience becomes part of the creation of the artwork. Their pieces provide instructions to the audience but offer themselves up as passive objects. But other artworks are explicitly collaborative and aimed at establishing an interactive creative process. Rainer's *Trio A* is a piece that she has transmitted to other dancers including non-professionals. It becomes a communal work, a practice that can be shaped collaboratively and participated in actively, *practised* and not merely received by, or acting on, others. Beuys understood his artworks to include discussions with audience members, for example in his *Directional Forces* (1974). This piece created stacks of blackboards drawn by Beuys but also involving the input and interventions of visitors. Caroline Tisdall recounts that '[t]he principle idea of *Directional Forces* was that the work should grow through the course of time and the intervention of visitors' (Tisdall 1998: 109). Participating in collaborative art practice such as dance or dialogue can be taken up by the audience as part of a hermeneutics of the self. Volker Harlan explains the context of a discussion with Joseph Beuys, which was, Harlan recounts part of a frequent gathering of a group of young people trying to understand 'the world, society and ourselves'.

> Essentially our questions related to how we should lead and shape our lives. It seemed natural therefore to concentrate not only on theoretical considerations but also to engage with specific, practical exercises. Such exercises were essentially artistic in character, and did not serve any immediate, external purpose. They did not serve to prepare an exhibition or a publication, but solely to 'come into movement' ourselves. To discover new forms and ways of living. And even if these forms were not new, they were at least self-discovered; for in discovering them ourselves they remain available to consciousness and can then – more or less – be implemented in all areas of practical life. (Beuys 2004: 5)

This summary by Harlan of the meetings he engaged in can be taken, I think, as a summary of how artistic practice, conceived broadly, can be incorporated into a hermeneutics of the self, as discovery of, but also making available for implementation, new forms and ways of living. Beuys claimed that every human being is an artist (Beuys 2004: 2). Speaking at the New School in 1974, he said he was there to speak about 'the whole question of potential, the possibility that everybody can do his own particular kind of art and work for the new social organization' (Beuys 1990: 8). Beuys sought to break down the boundaries of what we conceive of as art, advocating the possibility that social and political action can itself be conceived of as artistic action in his notion of Social Sculpture. This is a notion that I will return to in the Conclusion. Given that our self-construction operates in the context of the social and cultural world in which we operate, the possibilities of our self-construction are expanded not only by directly operating on ourselves through a variety of hermeneutic practices but also in the transformation of our social environment in which these practices operate. The boundaries between artistic practice, practices of self-construction and practices of social engagement are thus fluid.

NOTES

1. In fact on my reading, Nietzsche thinks we cannot live and act without beliefs or values, although these need not be consciously held. We, or drives that push us to act, are making a judgement that an action is worthwhile simply by acting. For instance, he writes: 'to live man must evaluate' (Nietzsche 1988: vol. 11, 181).
2. For more detailed analysis and defence of this reading of Nietzsche see my 'Scepticism and Self-transformation in Nietzsche – On the Uses and Disadvantages of a Comparison to Pyrrhonian Scepticism' (Mitcheson 2017) and 'The Experiment of Incorporating Unbounded Truth' (Mitcheson 2015).
3. This comment refers to Schneemann's decision to perform *Interior Scroll* at the Telluride Film Festival in 1977. She had been invited 'to introduce a program of erotic films by women' which she selected along with Stan Brackhage, but was 'dismayed to see our programme title as "The Erotic Woman"' (Scheemann 1997: 236).
4. Jarosi argues for a reading of the *Orgien Mysterien Theater* in terms of traumatic subjectivity, arguing that in Nitsch's six-day play: 'Immersion, in effect, produced an environment within which the viewer alternated between the experience of intensified and impaired consciousness' which is similar to a state induced by trauma. This, argues Jarosi, provides an opportunity of working through collective trauma. Jarosi thus defends Nitsch against the accusation that he is merely repeating the violence of Western civilisation; if there is acting out there is also working out (2013: 858).

Conclusion

I started this book by considering the complexity involved in encountering Goya's *The Disasters of War*. I suggested that this complexity both challenged the idea of a simple self and, in the very experience of tension or ambivalence that complicates our idea of the self, suggested that there is a self than can feel tensions and ambivalence. I have argued that such a self is constructed and maintained through various interpretative processes, processes which are affected by their interactions with each other and their integration in forming a self. A constructed self, understood as the unification of various corporeal processes, drive interpretations and activities, is able to take up various practices which in turn affect the nature of this unification. There is no simple or singular agency, but rather shifting loci of agential processes with their own directional tendencies and material constraints. But this complex agency can affect deliberate shaping and reshaping of the self. The hermeneutics of the self is thus a complex, continual and circular process, and not something that is ever final.

Foucault suggests that the hermeneutics of the self includes various technologies that operate on us, and that we are induced to take up and operate on ourselves, according to various power strategies. His analysis of our contemporary hermeneutics of the self is that it produces a subjugated self. Resistance to the dominant power structures therefore demands that we accept the task of refusing what we are (Foucault 1982: 785). I have argued this refusal is the refusal of being tied to any particular identity and is thus both a refusal of who we are, in the sense of being untied from particular identities, and of what we are in the sense of refusing to be reduced to or held to any fixed identity. But this is not a refusal of or escape from the hermeneutics of the self, without which there is no self. Rather if we want to be untied from our identities we need to both better understand the operation of the hermeneutics of the self, including the involvement of power strategies, and the diversity of practices it already incorporates, and to practise the hermeneutics of the self differently, incorporating a still wider range of practices.

The narrative theory of self-construction involves a restrictive view of how we are constructed and a prescriptive view of how we can be constructed. To reduce the construction of a self to the construction of plot is to simplify the agency involved, neglecting both the corporeality of the interpretative processes that can contribute to self-constructions, and their diversity. A broader understanding of, and actual practice of, the hermeneutics of the self than that of emplotment, which can do justice to the corporeality and multiplicity of interpretative processes that could and do contribute to self-construction, is thus required.

In order to elaborate a broader approach to the hermeneutics of the self, we must move away from a model of hermeneutics which is tied to the idea of a passive text in which we search for meaning. I have employed Nietzsche's insights to this effect. For Nietzsche, it is drives which interpret, and the activity and creation of the drives are modes of interpretation (Nietzsche 1988: vol. 9, 216; vol. 12, 315). Nietzsche's is an understanding of hermeneutics that encompasses the creation of concepts and values, the shaping of forms, the invention and take up of practices, and the cultivation of habits, and which ultimately understands these all as bodily activities. A hermeneutics of the self which takes this broad understanding of hermeneutics liberated from text allows that we can incorporate various interpretative activities and integrate competing interpretations. One can thus '"give style" to one's character', establishing and maintaining a self 'through long practice and daily work' (Nietzsche 2001: 163).

We have seen that visual art illustrates the operation of hermeneutics beyond the paradigm of text. Louise Bourgeois's sculptures demonstrated the possibility of incorporating diverse interpretations in one form, but also the need to work with the tendencies of the material, which have both a limit to their plasticity and their own unfolding processes. The model of self-construction we can draw from the example of such visual or plastic art practice is one in which there is no singular agent of construction but rather collaboration, accommodation and compromise between different processes and their trajectories. The form that emerges, both in the case of the artwork and that of a tenuously united self, is one that incorporates tensions and ambivalence, uniting as it does diverse processes.

It also incorporates cultural significations and operates within cultural constraints. We saw clearly with the example of Cindy Sherman's *Film Stills* how identity, the way we understand ourselves both as an individual and as participating in social roles and cultural tropes, can be constructed according to cultural codes. The significance of the image, and stylistic referents to media such as film, clearly show that self-construction incorporates technologies of the self beyond narrative. But a self reduced to either narrative or image is tied to what can be codified. Bodily activity, which can contribute to a hermeneutics of the self, exceeds representational capture. Artworks hint at the processes that escape representation by pushing the figure to its limits, as in Bacon's paintings. And they can find alternatives to representation that allow an exploration of a range of bodily processes. Engaging the audience through their reactions or active interventions and collaborations provides opportunities for unlearning and learning a variety of bodily practices and habits. Artworks can thus expand our hermeneutics of the self both by drawing our attention to, and exploring the possibilities of, a range of bodily processes that have been overlooked or deliberately excluded, and by physically affecting these processes. Thus, artworks can operate as technologies of the self which can be both critical and constructive. Artworks can take a critical perspective and work to untie us from a given cultural or political identity. But they can also allow us to both create new perspectives, as Nietzsche suggested to 'create eyes for ourselves' (Nietzsche 1988: vol. 9, 494–5), and to integrate different perspectives, forming new creative synthesises.

While I argued that narrative theories of the self are too narrow in their understanding of self-construction, neglecting the body and simplifying agency, I also acknowledged the strength of Ricoeur's account in noting the interdependence between the possibilities for selfhood and artistic and cultural creations. On the one hand, for Ricoeur the literary artwork is interpreted as a coherent work by a reader, 'the process of composition, of configuration, is not completed in the text but in the reader' (Ricoeur 1991a: 26). But on the other hand, this makes possible 'the reconfiguration of life by narrative' (Ricoeur 1991a: 26). Literature on Ricoeur's account can transfigure the reader. This makes artworks material that can be incorporated into our self-construction, and practices that expand the world of art also expand the possibilities of our hermeneutics of the self, which in turn expand the possibilities of art. In Ricoeur's narrative theory of the self, reading completes narrative configuration in a text, which provides possibilities for action, which in turn refigures the readers who take them up, whose lives prefigure the narratives that can be written. Once we are freed from tying the hermeneutics of the self to narrative and text alone, then we expand the enclosure of the circle connecting readers of text and authors of text to encompass the audience member's interpretations of a variety of artistic works. Berger suggests that 'the reciprocal nature of vision is more fundamental that that of spoken dialogue' and that '[s]eeing comes before words' (Berger 1972: 9, 7), while artworks that foreground touch or sound in turn challenge the pre-eminence of vision. A range of artworks, employing a range of senses and drives, expands our possibilities of self-construction; while new modes of self-construction, and new forms of selfhood, expand the possibilities of art. This is a continual process of the expansion and exploration of different interpretative perspectives.

Ricoeur's account recognises a circularity between self and culture, in which artworks can have an important effect on our self-construction, and our self-construction will in turn effect artworks. But the context in which we practise our hermeneutics of the self includes a wider environment that encompasses the social and natural world. The possibilities for action that Ricoeur refers to include how we act in relation to other people and other organisms. For Ricoeur, these actions are influenced by the models we find in literature and in turn influence literature. My account of the scope of a hermeneutics of the self expands this circle of mutual enhancement between self and art beyond literature to incorporate other art forms. But the circular model, while recognising the mutual influence between art on the one hand and selves and their actions on the other, still separates the world of the artwork and the world of non-artistic agency into distinct, if interdependent, spheres, linked by the tracing of circle.

Joseph Beuys suggests more than circular feedback in his concept of 'Social Sculpture'. Social action for Beuys is a form of artistic practice, on this model the spheres of subject, action and art are porous. Social Sculpture for Beuys is 'how we mold and shape the world in which we live' (Beuys 1990: 21). To understand Social Sculpture, we must understand that for Beuys sculpture contrasts to carving and works from the inside 'building up processes' (Beuys 2004: 61). Describing his artworks, Beuys says 'the nature of my sculpture is not fixed and finished. Processes continue in most of them: chemical reactions, fermentations, colour changes, decay, drying up' (Beuys 1990: 19). *Butter Pots* (1983), for instance, consisted of two stags' skulls containing butter, which inevitably will go rancid over time. Beuys makes connections between the materials of his sculptures, and their fluid changing nature, and our corporeal processes. For example, of his *Fat Chair* (1963) he writes: 'the chair represents a kind of human anatomy, the area of digestive and excretive warmth processes, sexual organs and interesting chemical change' (Beuys 1990: 125). Thus, Social Sculpture, like his own sculptural pieces, involves – as does, I have argued, self-construction

– multiple and continuous material processes. The processes that form the structure of society connect to the multiple and continuous material processes of the bodies of social actors. Social Sculpture consists of actively and creatively shaping our world in ways that are responsive to its materiality, this materiality includes the corporeality of social actors and the natural environment on which they are dependent. Given our intersubjectivity and our dependence on our environment, engaging in practices which change the world around us is continuous with our hermeneutics of the self.

We have seen that refusing what we are requires more than a critical awareness of the social and political forces at work in shaping us, and a detachment from existing identities. It also requires creative experimentation with what we can be. Foucault may be right that this refusal of what we are is a necessary part of social and political resistance (Foucault 1982: 785), but the latter, understood to involve creative activity, is also integral to the possibility of this refusal. In this book, I have focused on self-construction, but this is not isolated from construction of the cultural and social world in which selves are constructed and operate. The creation of alternative identities and experimentation with alternative ways of relating to our identity or identities, and thus of being a self, is limited by the context in which self-construction operates. Creative self-construction thus incorporates creative action that shapes this context. New ways of relating to our identity can also involve new ways of relating to others, and to the environment, both cultural and natural.

With his *7,000 Oaks* (1982–6) Beuys undertook to plant 7,000 oak trees; 7,000 basalt columns were piled up in the main square of Kassel each to be placed with a newly planted oak tree. With such a large number of trees he aimed to make a significant environmental impact and to inspire future tree plantings. In an interview with Richard Demarco, Beuys put this action in the context of 'regenerative activity; it will be a therapy for all the problems we are standing before' (Beuys 1990: 110). I end with this ambitious, idealistic vision of art espoused by Beuys because any project of self-construction – which may employ artworks as technologies of the self, which model, reveal and affect various bodily processes which contribute to this self-construction – must recognise that this will always operate in the context of the social and natural world. A hermeneutics of the self, therefore, has no clearly defined boundaries, but incorporates our interpretations of and impact on the world around us.

List of Artworks Referenced

Abramović, Marina
(1974) *Rhythm O*, performance.

Bacon, Francis
(1962) *Three Studies for a Crucifixion*, triptych, oil on canvas, each 198 × 145 cm.
(1964) *Three Figures in a Room*, oil on canvas, each 198 × 147.5 cm.
(1973, May–June) *Triptych*, oil on canvas, 198 × 147 cm.
(1975) *Three Figures and Portrait*, oil paint and pastel on canvas, 198.1 × 147.3 cm.

Beuys, Joseph
(1974) *Directional Forces*, interactive installations with blackboards, created at the ICA London.
(1963) *Fat Chair*, wooden chair, fat, wax, metal wire, 90 × 30 × 30 cm.
(1982–6) *7,000 Oaks*, a project initiated in 1982 for Documenta 7 to plant 7,000 oaks, each with a basalt stone.
(1983) *Butter Pots*, two stags' skulls filled with butter.

Bourgeois, Louise
(1962) *Clutching*, plaster, 30.5 × 33 × 30.5 cm.
(1963–5) *Amoeba*, bronze, painted white, wall piece, 95.3 × 72.4 × 33.7 cm.
(1967) *Soft Landscape I*, pigmented resin, 10.2 × 30.45 × 27.9 cm.
— *Soft Landscape II*, carved alabaster, 17.4 × 37.1 × 24.4 cm.
(1968) *Fillette*, latex over plaster, 59.5 × 27.9 × 19.1 cm.
— *Janus Fleuri*, bronze, gold patina, 25.7 × 31.8 × 21.3 cm.
(1968–9) *Avenza*, latex and fibreglass, 53.3 × 76.2 × 116.8 cm.
— *Avenza Revisited*, bronze, silver nitrate and polished patina, 43.2 × 104.1 × 88.9 cm.
— *Avenza Revisited II*, plaster, shellac, paint, plastic and wire on wood base, 140.9 × 141.9 × 240 cm.
(1969) *Cumul I*, marble, 56.8 × 127 × 121.9 cm.

(1974) *Destruction of the Father*, latex, plaster, wood, fabric and red light, 237.8 × 362.3 × 248 cm.
(1984) *Blind Man's Bluff*, marble, 92.7 × 88.9 × 63.5 cm.
— *Spiral Woman*, bronze, hanging piece, with slate disc, bronze, 48.2 × 10.2 × 14 cm; slate disc 3.1 × 86.3 × 86.3 cm.
(1994) *Femme Maison*, white marble, 11.4 × 31.1 × 6.6 cm.
(1998) *Three Horizontals*, fabric and steel, 134.6 × 182.9 × 91.4 cm.
(1999) *Maman*, bronze, stainless steel and marble, 927.1 × 891.5 × 1023.6 cm.
— *Do Not Abandon Me*, fabric and thread, 12.1 × 52.1 × 21.6 cm.
(2001) *Seven in Bed*, fabric and stainless steel, 29.2 × 53.3 × 53.3 cm.
(2002) *The Woven Child*, fabric and thread, 27.9 × 73.7 × 36.8 cm.
— *The Woven Child*, fabric and thread, 35.6 × 68.6 × 35.6 cm.
— *Fragile Goddess*, fabric, 31.8 × 12.7 × 15.2 cm.
(2003) *Spiral Woman*, fabric hanging piece, 175.3 × 36.5 × 34.3 cm.
— *Oedipus*, fabric, stainless steel, wood, glass: ten elements, 177.9 × 182.9 × 91.4 cm.
— *The Reticent Child*, fabric, marble, stainless steel and aluminium: six elements, 182.9 × 284.5 × 91.4 cm.

Boyce, Sonia
(1987) *From Tarzan to Rambo: English Born 'Native' Considers her Relationship to the Constructed/Self Image and her Roots in Reconstruction*, photographs, black and white, on paper, photocopies on paper, acrylic paint, ballpoint pen, crayon and felt-tip pen, support: 125 × 360 cm.

Cahun, Claude
(1919) *Self-portrait (in Profile, Wearing Corduroy Jacket)*, silver gelatin print, 23.8 × 17.9 cm.
(1927) *'I am in Training Don't Kiss Me'* series, silver gelatin print, 11.6 × 7.4 cm.
(1928) *Self-portrait (Reflected Image in Mirror with Chequered Jacket)*, gelatin silver print, 25.5 × 20.1 cm.
(1929) *Self-portrait (as Elle in Barbe-Bleue)*, silver gelatin print, 23.5 × 17.9 cm.
(1929) *Self-portrait (Double Head Image as Elle in Barbe-Bleue)*, silver gelatin print, 13.8 × 8.6 cm.
(1938) *Self-portrait (in Window of La Rocquaise)*, silver gelatin print, 11 × 9 cm.

Duchamp, Marcel
(1917) *Fountain*, ready-made, porcelain urinal, 61 cm × 36 cm × 48 cm.

Goya y Lucientes, Francisco de
(completed 1810–20, published 1863) *The Disasters of War*, plate no. 37, *This is Worse (Esto es peor)* (completed 1812–15), etching, lavis and drypoint on paper, 15.5 × 20.5 cm.

Hatoum, Mona
(1989) *The Light at the End*, angel iron frame, six heating elements, 166 × 162 × 5 cm.
(1994) *Corps Étranger*, video installation with cylindrical wooden structure, video projector, video player, amplifier, four speakers, 350 × 300 × 300 cm.
(1999) *Home*, wooden table, 15 steel kitchen utensils, electric wire, 3 light bulbs, software and audio, 600 × 350 cm.
(2008) *Day Bed*, black finished steel, 31 × 219 × 98 cm.

Horn, Rebecca
(1972) *Performances II*, film, 16 mm, shown as video, colour and sound.

McQueen, Steve
(1993) *Bear*, film, 16 mm, shown as video, projection, black and white, 9 mins 2 secs.

Nitsch, Hermann
(1998) *6-Tage-Spiel*, six-day action, Prinzendorf.

Ono, Yoko
(1964) *Cut Piece*, performance.

ORLAN
(1965) *Attempting to Escape the Frame with Mask No. 3*, gelatin silver print, 7 × 11.1 cm.
(1990–5) *Re-incarnation of Saint ORLAN*, nine performance surgeries.

Paxton, Steve and Rainer, Yvonne
(1963) *Word Words*, performance, Judson Church, New York.

Rainer, Yvonne
(1978) *Trio A*, video (black and white, sound), 10:21 mins.

Schneemann, Carloee
(1963) *Eye Body: 36 Transformative Actions for Camera*, paint, glue, fur, feathers, garden snakes, glass, plastic with the studio installation 'Big Boards'. Photographs by Icelandic artist Erró, on 35 mm black and white film.
(1963) *Meat Joy*, group performance, Paris.
(1975) *Interior Scroll*, performance, East Hampton, New York.

Sherman, Cindy
(1978) *Untitled Film Still #12*, gelatin silver print, 19.1 × 24 cm.
— *Untitled Film Still #13*, gelatin silver print, 25.4 × 20.3 cm.
— *Untitled Film Still #16*, gelatin silver print, 24 × 19.2 cm.

(1979) *Untitled Film Still #40*, gelatin silver print, 17.9 × 24 cm.
(1980) *Untitled Film Still #54*, gelatin silver print, 25.4 × 20.3 cm.
(1980) *Untitled Film Still #83*, gelatin silver print, 25.4 × 20.3 cm.
(1985) *Untitled #140*, chromogenic print, 184.2 × 125.4 cm.
(1985) *Untitled #156*, chromogenic print, 123.2 × 181.6 cm.
(1987) *Untitled #235*, chromogenic print, flush-mounted on board, 126.2 × 149.8 cm.
(1987) *Untitled #236*, colour photograph, 228.6 × 152.4 cm.

Bibliography

Ades, Dawn (2017), 'Claude Cahun's "Self-portraits"', in S. Howgate and D. Ades, *Gillian Wearing and Claude Cahun: Behind the Mask Another Mask*, London: National Portrait Gallery Publications, pp. 174–87.

Ansell-Pearson, Keith and Duncan Large (2006), *The Nietzsche Reader*, Malden, MA: Blackwell.

Archer, Michael, Guy Brett, M. Catherine de Zegher and Nancy Spector (2016), *Mona Hatoum*, London: Phaidon Press Ltd.

Berger, John (1972), *Ways of Seeing*, London: British Broadcasting Corporation and Penguin Books.

Beuys, Joseph (1990), *Energy Plan for the Western Man: Writings and Interviews with the Artist*, ed. C. Kuoni, New York: Four Walls Eight Windows.

— (2004), *What is Art?*, ed. V. Harlan, trans. M. Barton and S. Sacks, West Hoathly: Clairview Books.

Bickers, Patricia (1996), 'Let's Get Physical (Interview with Steve McQueen)', *Art Monthly*, 202: 1–5.

Borzello, Frances (2016), *Seeing Ourselves; Women's Self-Portraits*, London: Thames and Hudson Ltd.

Bourgeois, Louise (1998), *Destruction of the Father Reconstruction of the Father: Writings and Interviews, 1923–1997*, ed. M. Bernadac and H. Obrist, London: Violette Editions.

— (2012), *The Return of the Repressed, Vol. II: Psychoanalytic Writings*, ed. P. Laratt-Smith, London: Violette Editions.

Brandon, Priscilla (2016), 'Body and Self: An Entangled Narrative', *Phenomenology and Cognitive Science*, 15: 67–83.

Bryan-Wilson, Julia (2012), 'Practicing "Trio" A', *October*, 140: 54–74.

Bryson, Norman (2006), 'House of Wax (1993)', in J. Burton (ed.), *October Files 6; Cindy Sherman*, Cambridge, MA and London: The MIT Press, pp. 83–96.

Cahun, Claude (2007), *Disavowals: Or Cancelled Confessions*, trans. S. de Muth, London: Tate Publishing.

Carr, David, Charles Taylor and Paul Ricoeur (1991), 'Discussion: Ricoeur on

Narrative', in D. Wood (ed.), *On Paul Ricoeur: Narrative and Interpretation*, London: Routledge, pp. 160–87.

Colwell, C. (1994), 'The Retreat of the Subject in the Late Foucault', *Philosophy Today*, 38(1): 56–69.

Cowie, Elizabeth (2000), 'Woman as Signifier', in E. A. Kaplan (ed.), *Feminism and Film*, Oxford: Oxford University Press, pp. 48–65.

Coxon, Anne (2007a), 'Avenza', in F. Morris (ed.), *Louise Bourgeois*, London: Tate Gallery Publications, p. 52.

— (2007b), 'Soft Landscape', in F. Morris (ed.), *Louise Bourgeois*, London: Tate Gallery Publications, p. 272.

— (2010), *Louise Bourgeois*, London: Tate Publishing.

Davey, Nicholas (2002), 'Hermeneutics and Art Theory', in P. Smith and C. Wilde (eds), *A Companion to Art Theory*, Oxford: Blackwell Publishers, pp. 436–47.

Deleuze, Giles (2017), *Francis Bacon: The Logic of Sensation*, trans. D. W. Smith, London and New York: Bloomsbury.

Dennett, Daniel, C. (1992), 'The Self as the Centre of Narrative Gravity', in P. M. Cole, F. S. Kessel and D. J. Johnson (eds), *Self and Consciousness: Multiple Perspectives*, Hillsdale, NJ: Lawrence Erlbaum Associates, pp. 103–15.

Descartes, René (2017), *Meditations on First Philosophy with Selections from the Objections and Replies*, trans. and ed. J. Cottingham, Cambridge: Cambridge University Press.

Foucault, Michel (1978), *History of Sexuality, Vol. 1: The Will to Knowledge*, trans. R. Hurley, New York: Random House.

— (1982), 'The Subject and Power', *Critical Inquiry*, 8(4): 777–95.

— (1985), *History of Sexuality, Vol. 2: The Use of Pleasure*, trans. R. Hurley, New York: Random House.

— (1986), *The History of Sexuality, Vol. 3: The Care of the Self*, trans. R. Hurley, New York: Random House.

— (1988), 'Technologies of the Self', in H. Gutman, P. H. Hutton and L. H. Martin (eds), *Technologies of the Self: A Seminar with Michel Foucault*, Amherst: University of Massachusetts Press, pp. 16–49.

— (1991), 'Governmentality', in G. Burchell, C. Gordon and P. Miller (eds), *The Foucault Effect*, London: Harvester Wheatsheaf.

— (1993), 'About the Beginnings of the Hermeneutics of the Self: Two Lectures at Dartmouth', *Political Theory*, 21(2): 198–227.

— (1994), 'Entretien avec Michel Foucault', in D. Defert and F. Ewald (eds), *Dis et écrits 1954–1988: IV 1980–1988*, Paris: Callimard, pp. 41–95.

— (1995), *Discipline and Punish*, trans. A. Sheridan, New York: Vintage Books.

— (1997), 'The Ethics for the Concern for Self as a Practice of Freedom', in Paul Rabinow (ed.), *Essential Works of Foucault 1954–1984: Volume 1, Ethics, Subjectivity and Truth*, London: Penguin, pp. 281–301.

— (2005), *The Hermeneutics of the Subject: Lectures at the Collège de France 1981–1982*, trans. G. Burchell, New York: Picado.

Freud, Sigmund (2001 [1956–74]), *The Standard Edition of the Complete Psychological Works of Sigmund Freud*, translated from the German under the general editorship of J. Strachey, in collaboration with A. Freud, assisted by A. Strachey and A. Tyson (eds), London: Hogarth.

Goldie, Peter (2012), *The Mess Inside; Narrative, Emotion, and the Mind*, Oxford: Oxford University Press.

Greenblatt, Stephen (1980), *Renaissance Self-Fashioning*, Chicago and London: The University of Chicago Press.

Haenlein, Carl (1997), *Rebecca Horn: The Glance of Infinity*, Zürich and New York: Scalo.

Heidegger, Martin (1991), *Nietzsche*, trans. D. F. Krell, New York: Harper San Francisco.

Herkenhoff, Paulo (2007), 'Diary', in F. Morris (ed.), *Louise Bourgeois*, London: Tate Gallery Publications, p. 104.

Hofmeyr, Brenda (2006), 'The Power Not to Be (What We Are): The Politics and Ethics of Self-Creation in Foucault', *Journal of Moral Philosophy: An International Journal of Moral, Political and Legal Philosophy*, 2: 215–30.

Honoré, Vincent (2007), 'Blind Man's Bluff', in F. Morris (ed.), *Louise Bourgeois*, London: Tate Gallery Publications, p. 58.

Irigaray, Luce (1985), *This Sex Which Is Not One*, trans. C. Porter, New York: Cornell University Press.

Jarosi, Susan (2013), 'Traumatic Subjectivity and the Continuum of History: Hermann Nitsch's *Orgies Mysteries Theater*', *Art History*, 36(4): 834–65.

Jones, Amelia (1998), *Body Art/Performing the Subject*, Minneapolis: University of Minnesota Press.

Krauss, Rosalind (2000), *Bachelors*, Cambridge, MA and London: The MIT Press.

— (2006), 'Cindy Sherman: Untitled (1993)', in J. Burton (ed.), *October Files 6: Cindy Sherman*, Cambridge, MA and London: The MIT Press, pp. 83–96.

— (2007), 'Fillette', in M. Frances (ed.), *Louise Bourgeois*, London: Tate Gallery Publications, p. 146.

Kristeva, Julia (2007), 'Runaway Girl: Louise Bourgeois: From "Little Pea" to Runaway Girl', in M. Frances (ed.), London: Tate Gallery Publications, pp. 246–52.

Kuspit, Donald (1988), *Bourgeois (An Interview with Louise Bourgeois)*, New York: Vintage Books.

Laplanche, Jean and Jean-Bertrand Pontalis (1973), *The Language of Psychoanalysis*, London: Hogarth Press.

Lehrer, Ronald (1995), *Nietzsche's Presence in Freud's Life and Thought*, Albany: State University of New York Press.

Lippard, Lucy (1975), 'From the Inside Out', *Art Forum*, 13 (9): 26–33.

Lotz, Christian (2017), *The Art of Gerhard Richter: Hermeneutics, Images, Meaning*, London: Bloomsbury.

MacIntyre, Alasdair (2007 [1985]), *After Virtue: A Study in Moral Theory*, London: Duckworth.

Mackenzie, Catriona (2009), 'Personal Identity, Narrative Integration, and Embodiment', in S. Campbell, L. Meynell and S. Sherwin (eds), *Embodiment and Agency*, University Park, PA: Penn State University Press, pp. 100–25.

— (2014), 'Embodied Agents, Narrative Selves', *Philosophical Explorations*, 17 (2): 154–71.

Marion-Young, Iris (1990), *Throwing Like a Girl: And Other Essays in Feminist Philosophy and Social Theory*, Bloomington: Indiana University Press.

Merleau-Ponty, Maurice (2012), *Phenomenology of Perception*, trans. D. A. Landes, Abingdon and New York: Routledge.

Meyers, Diana Tietjens (2002), *Gender in the Mirror*, New York: Oxford University Press.

— (2013), 'Corporeal Selfhood, Self-interpretation, and Narrative Selfhood', *Philosophical Explorations: An International Journal for the Philosophy of Mind and Action*, 17 (2): 141–53.

Midgley, Nicholas (2006), 'Re-reading "Little Hans": Freud's Case Study and the Question of Competing Paradigms in Psychoanalysis', *Journal of the American Psychanalytic Association*, 54 (2): 537–59.

Mitcheson, Katrina (2013), *Nietzsche, Truth and Transformation*, Basingstoke: Palgrave Macmillan.

— (2015), 'The Experiment of Incorporating Unbounded Truth', in R. Bamford (ed.), *Nietzsche's Free Spirit Philosophy*, Lanham, MD: Rowman and Littlefield International, pp. 139–156.

— (2017), 'Scepticism and Self-transformation in Nietzsche – On the Uses and Disadvantages of a Comparison to Pyrrhonian Scepticism', *British Journal for the History of Philosophy*, 25 (1): 63–83.

Moore, Gregory (2002), *Nietzsche, Biology, and Metaphor*, Cambridge: Cambridge University Press.

Morris, Frances (2007), *Louise Bourgeois*, London: Tate Gallery Publications.

Müller-Lauter, Wolfgang (1999), *Nietzsche: His Philosophy of Contradictions and the Contradictions of his Philosophy*, trans. D. J. Parent, Urbana: University of Illinois Press.

Musil, Robert (1995), *The Man Without Qualities*, trans. S. Wilkins and B. Pike, London: Picador.

Nehamas, Alexander (1985), *Nietzsche: Life as Literature*, Cambridge, MA and London: Harvard University Press.

Nietzsche, Friedrich (1986), *Human, All Too Human*, trans. R. J. Hollingdale, Cambridge and New York: Cambridge University Press.

— (1988), *Sämtliche Werke: Kritische Studienausgabe in 15 Einzelbänden*, ed. G. Colli and M. Montinari, München: Deutscher Taschenbuch Verlag.

— (1997), *Untimely Meditations*, trans. R. J. Hollingdale, Cambridge and New York: Cambridge University Press.

— (1999), *The Birth of Tragedy and Other Writings*, trans. R. Speirs, ed. R. Geuss and R. Speirs, Cambridge: Cambridge University Press.

— (2001), *Gay Science: With a Prelude in German Rhymes and an Appendix of Songs*, trans. J. Nauckhoff and A. Del Caro, ed. B Williams, Cambridge: Cambridge University Press.

— (2002), *Beyond Good and Evil*, trans. J. Norman, ed. R. Horstmann and J. Norman, Cambridge: Cambridge University Press.

— (2005a), *The Anti-Christ, Ecce Homo, Twilight of the Idols, and Other Writings*, trans. J. Norman, ed. A. Ridley and J. Norman, Cambridge: Cambridge University Press.

— (2005b), *Thus Spoke Zarathustra: A Book for Everyone and Nobody*, trans. G. Parkes, Oxford: Oxford University Press.

— (2007), *On the Genealogy of Morality*, trans. C. Diethe, ed. K. Ansell-Pearson, New York: Cambridge University Press.

Nitsch, Hermann (n.d., a), 'The Orgies Mysteries Theatre', accessed 16 February 2020 at: https://www.nitsch.org/en/aktionen/

— (n.d., b), 'Publications', accessed 16 February 2020 at: https://www.nitsch.org/en/en_publications/

Nixon, Mignon (2005), *Fantastic Reality: Louise Bourgeois and a Story of Modern Art*, Cambridge, MA and London: The MIT Press.

O'Leary, Timothy (2002), *Foucault and the Art of Ethics*, London: Continuum.

Plato (1997), *Complete Works*, ed. J. M. Cooper and D. S. Hutchinson, Indianapolis and Cambridge: Hackett Publishing Company.

Poellner, Peter (1995), *Nietzsche and Metaphysics*, Oxford: Clarendon Press.

Pollock, Griselda (1988), *Vision and Difference: Femininity, Feminism and Histories of Art*, London and New York: Routledge.

Rasmussen, David M. (1995), 'Rethinking Subjectivity: Narrative Identity and the Self', *Philosophy and Social Criticism*, 21 (5–6): 159–72.

Richardson, John (1996), *Nietzsche's System*, New York: Oxford University Press.

Ricoeur, Paul (1970), *Freud and Philosophy: An Essay on Interpretation*, trans. D. Savage, New Haven, CT and London: Yale University Press.

— (1973), 'The Model of the Text: Meaningful Action Considered as a Text', *New Literary History*, 5 (1): 91–117.

— (1984), *Time and Narrative 1*, trans. K. McLaughlin and D. Pellauer, Chicago: University of Chicago Press.

— (1985), *Time and Narrative 2*, trans. K. McLaughlin and D. Pellauer, Chicago: University of Chicago Press.

— (1988), *Time and Narrative 3*, trans. K. Blamey and D. Pellauer, Chicago: University of Chicago Press.

— (1991a), 'Life in Quest of Narrative', in D. Wood (ed.), *On Paul Ricoeur: Narrative and Interpretation*, London: Routledge, pp. 20–33.

— (1991b), 'Narrative Identity', in D. Wood (ed.), *On Paul Ricoeur: Narrative and Interpretation*, London: Routledge, pp. 188–9.

— (1992), *Oneself as Another*, trans. K. Blamey, Chicago and London: University of Chicago Press.

Sartre, Jean Paul (2003), *Being and Nothingness*, trans. H. E. Barnes, Abingdon: Routledge.

Sayers, Henry M. (1989), *The Object of Performance: The American Avant-Garde Since 1970*, Chicago and London: University of Chicago Press.

Schechtman, Marya (2011), 'The Narrative Self', in S. Gallagher (ed.), *The Oxford Handbook of the Self*, Oxford: Oxford University Press, pp. 394–416.

Schneemann, Carolee (1997), *More Than Meat Joy: Complete Performance Works & Selected Writings*, Kingston, New York: McPherson & Company.

Schrift, Alan (1995), *Nietzsche's French Legacy: A Genealogy of Poststructuralism*, Abingdon and New York: Routledge.

Strawson, Galen (2004), 'Against Narrativity', *Ratio*, 17 (4): 428–52.

Sylvester, David (1980 [1975]), *Francis Bacon*, London: Thames & Hudson.

Taylor, Charles (1992), *Sources of the Self: Making of Modern Identity*, Cambridge: Cambridge University Press.

Teichert, Dieter (2004), 'Narrative, Identity and the Self', *Journal of Consciousness Studies*, 11 (10–11): 175–91.

Tisdall, Caroline (1998), *Joseph Beuys: We Go this Way*, London: Violette Editions.

van Alphen, Ernst (1993), *Francis Bacon and the Loss of Self*, Cambridge, MA: Harvard University Press.

Venema, Henry Isaac (2000), *Identify Selfhood: Imagination, Narrative, and Hermeneutics in the Thought of Paul Ricoeur*, Albany: State University of New York Press.

Vollmer, Fred (2005), 'The Narrative Self', *Journal for the Theory of Social Behaviour*, 35 (2): 189–205.

Warr, Tracey and Amelia Jones (2000), *The Artist's Body*, London: Phaidon.

Williamson, Judith (2006), 'A Piece of the Action: Images of "Woman" in the Photography of Cindy Sherman (1991)', in J. Burton (ed.), *October Files 6: Cindy Sherman*, Cambridge, MA and London: The MIT Press, pp. 83–96.

Wollheim, Richard (1991), *Freud*, London: Fontana Press.

Wood, David (1991), 'Introduction: Interpreting Narrative', in D. Wood (ed.), *On Paul Ricoeur: Narrative and Interpretation*, London: Routledge, pp. 1–19.

Wye, Deborah (2017), *Louise Bourgeois: An Unfolding Portrait: Prints, Books, and the Creative Process*, New York: Museum of Modern Art.

Zahavi, Dan (2007), 'Self and Other: The Limits of Narrative Understanding (Series: Narrative and Understanding Persons)', *Royal Institute of Philosophy Supplement*, 60: 179–201.

Index